DATE DUE

OC 15 02			

DEMCO 38-296

KAHLIL GIBRAN OF LEBANON

KAHLIL GIBRAN
OF LEBANON

A re-evaluation of the life and works of
the author of
The Prophet

Suheil Bushrui

COLIN SMYTHE
Gerrards Cross 1987

Copyright © 1987 by Suheil Bushrui

Colin Smythe Limited
Buckinghamshire

British Library Cataloguing in Publication Data

Bushrui, Suheil Badi'
    Kahlil Gibran : a re-evaluation
of the life and works of the author of
                The Prophet.
    1. Gibran, Kahlil, *1883–1931* —Criticism
             and interpretation
                  I. Title
        892' 715   PJ7826.I2Z/
        ISBN 0–86140–279–0

Produced in Great Britain
Set by Grove Graphics, Tring, Herts.
and printed and bound by Billing & Sons Ltd., Worcester

FOR

ALL THOSE WHO HAVE GENEROUSLY SPONSORED
THE KAHLIL GIBRAN DISTINGUISHED CHAIR AT THE
UNIVERSITY OF MARYLAND, AND IN PARTICULAR TO
EDWIN ABELA, CHAIRMAN OF ITS INTERNATIONAL
ADVISORY BOARD, IN RECOGNITION OF HIS GENEROUS
SUPPORT OF THE ARTS AND THE PUBLICATION OF
THIS BOOK.

"Even were Lebanon not my country, I would choose
it for my country."

Kahlil Gibran

"My heart is capable of every form:
A cloister for the monk, a fane for idols,
A pasture for gazelles, the votary's Ka'ba,
The tables of the Torah, the Koran,
Love is the faith I hold; wherever turn
His camels, still the one true faith is mine."

Muhi'l-Din ibn al-'Arabi
(translated by *R. A. Nicholson*)

"You are my brother and I love you;
I love you
at prayer in your mosque,
at your worship in your temple,
at your devotions in your church;
for you and I are the sons of one religion –
the spirit."

Kahlil Gibran

"Poetry can be to Man what love is to the hero.
She can neither advise him, nor strike blows on
his behalf, nor do any other office for him. But
she can educate him to be a hero. She can summon
him to action and furnish him with strength for
all that he ought to be."

Friedrich Schiller
(translated by *Reginald Snell*)

TABLE OF CONTENTS

ACKNOWLEDGEMENTS

In the preparation of this volume I have received much valuable help from Dr Geoffrey Nash, Dr James Malarky, Mr Charles Lewis, Professor Nadim Naimy, Professor Edward Azar, and the poets Francis Warner and F. T. Prince, each of whom has been involved in reading the text and giving advice. Any shortcomings or mistakes, however, are entirely my responsibility.

Acknowledgement is hereby extended to Alfred A. Knopf Inc. for permission to reprint material from the following books by Kahlil Gibran:

— *The Madman:* Copyright 1918 by Kahlil Gibran. Renewal copyright 1946 by Administrators C.T.A. of Kahlil Gibran Estate and Mary G. Gibran.
— *The Forerunner:* Copyright 1920 by Kahlil Gibran. Renewal copyright 1948 by Administrators C.T.A. of Kahlil Gibran Estate and Mary G. Gibran.
— *The Prophet:* Copyright 1923 by Kahlil Gibran. Renewal copyright 1951 by Administrators C.T.A. of Kahlil Gibran Estate and Mary G. Gibran.
— *Sand and Foam:* Copyright 1926 by Kahlil Gibran. Renewal copyright 1954 by Administrators C.T.A. of Kahlil Gibran Estate and Mary G. Gibran.
— *Jesus, the Son of Man:* Copyright 1928 by Kahlil Gibran. Renewal copyright 1956 by Administrators C.T.A. of Kahlil Gibran Estate and Mary G. Gibran.
— *The Earth Gods:* Copyright 1931 by Kahlil Gibran. Renewal copyright 1959 by Administrators C.T.A. of Kahlil Gibran Estate and Mary G. Gibran.

11

INTRODUCTION

Kahlil Gibran: a Lebanese Identity

This study is intended as a concise guide for the Gibran scholar and for anyone who has become acquainted with the unique spirit of Gibran's works. Several biographical works have been published but none can claim to be definitive, mainly because criticism of his work has so far failed to establish genuine criteria owing to the special East/West synthesis that his writing represents. It is therefore time for a radical reassessment of Gibran, whose place in world literature is truly unique. Indeed, such a reassessment is not only long overdue, but of striking relevance to the times in which we live.

The first half of the book is devoted to significant events of Gibran's life, and provides the necessary background to his writing and painting, with particular reference to the individuals and writings that appear to have influenced him most strongly. These are further explored in the second half, which is a critical study of his work and his contribution to world literature.

There is an extraordinary diversity of critical opinion as to the literary and philosophical worth of Gibran's English works in particular. Those who have blindly worshipped Gibran, as if one needed only to read *The Prophet* for the problems of life to vanish away like magic, have done him as much disservice as those who have pilloried him for his unfashionable emphasis on tolerance and compassion. Few have appreciated the essentially Lebanese character of Gibran the man and Gibran the poet.

The role of the poet as the voice of his nation is a tradition exemplified by great men like Goethe and Yeats. Although he passed almost the whole of his adult life in America, Gibran was permeated with the spirit of his native Lebanon. The closest parallel here is James Joyce (born eleven months before Gibran), whose self-imposed exile only lent greater poignancy to the quintessential Irishness in his writings. Gibran never forgot the enormous debt he owed to America, but while exhorting his fellow Lebanese exiles to acknowledge that debt he stressed that they should in no way feel intimidated by the achievements of their adopted country. 'Remember,' he said,

when you stand before the towers of New York and Washington, Chicago and San Franciso, that your ancestors built Damascus and Byblos, and Tyre and Sidon and Antioch. Be proud that you are Americans, but be proud also that your fathers and mothers came from a land upon which God laid His gracious hand, and raised His messengers.[1]

As he grew steadily more famous and prosperous in America, Gibran's longing for his homeland of Lebanon became a near-obsession which asserted itself almost whenever he put pen to paper. Even when he was not referring directly to Lebanon, he would consciously adopt a mode of thought and expression that was uniquely Lebanese. As early as 1908 he wrote to his friend Ameen Guraieb, who had travelled from America to Lebanon, with this heartfelt request:

When you are in a beautiful spot or among learned people, or by the side of old ruins, or on the top of a high mountain, whisper my name so that my soul will go to Lebanon and hover around you and share with you the pleasure of life and all life's meanings and secrets. Remember me when you see the sun rising from behind Mount Sunnin or Fam el Mizab. Think of me when you see the sun coming down toward its setting, spreading its red garment upon the mountains and the valleys as if shedding blood instead of tears as it bids Lebanon farewell. Recall my name when you see the shepherds sitting in the shadow of the trees and blowing their reeds and filling the silent field with soothing music as did Apollo when he was exiled to this world. Think of me when you see the damsels carrying their earthenware jars filled with water upon their shoulders. Remember me when you see the Lebanese villager ploughing the earth before the face of the sun, with beads of sweat adorning his forehead while his back is bent under the heavy duty of labour. Remember me when you hear the songs and hymns that Nature has woven from the sinews of moonlight, mingled with the aromatic scent of the valleys, mixed with the frolicsome breeze of the Holy Cedars, and poured into the hearts of the Lebanese.[2]

The many historical and legendary associations in the countryside around his birthplace were a source of great wonder to Gibran. An early poem entitled 'Communion of Spirits' contains a powerful reference to some of the succeeding civilizations that shaped Lebanon:

> The phantoms of past ages walk in the valleys,
> On the heights the spirits of kings and
> prophets wander.
> My thoughts have turned towards the places of
> remembrance
> And shewn to me the might of Chaldea and the
> Assyrian's pride and Arabia's nobility.

The same poem also describes characteristic sounds of the countryside 'bringing to our ears Solomon's Song, and the strains of David's lyre'.[3]

The Bible, with its references to Lebanon and its Cedars, influenced Gibran more than any other book. He was reared as a Maronite Christian, and the form of English he used in *The Prophet, Jesus, the Son of Man* and other mature writings is consciously modelled on that of the King James Authorised Version. The Bible uses the name given to the country of Gibran's birth as a synonym for beauty in the Song of Solomon (v.15): 'His countenance is as Lebanon, excellent as the cedars.' In Psalm 104 (v.16), it is recorded that 'the trees of the Lord are full of sap; the cedars of Lebanon, which He hath planted'. In *Jesus, the Son of Man*, Gibran puts a similar reference into the mouth of Jesus, as reported by Rumanous, a Greek poet:

Oftentimes I have seen Him bending down to touch the blades of grass. And in my heart I have heard Him say: 'Little green things, you shall be with me in my kingdom, even as the oaks of Basan, and the cedars of Lebanon'.[4]

Every nation has as part of its heritage an heroic myth or legend which has inspired it. The Irish, for example, have the figure of Cuchulain, whose name and mighty deeds are a symbol of national consciousness and aspiration. It matters little whether Cuchulain was a real person or a purely mythological creation, only what he represents to Ireland. For Christians in Lebanon it is Jesus Christ who embodies this peculiar 'mythological' significance, as a leader of men who not only taught a gospel of great wisdom and compassion, but died on the cross for his beliefs, refusing to combat ignorance and intolerance with weapons other than peaceful ones.

Gibran was imbued with the spirit of this mythology, as well as that of the Sufi tradition which influenced him through the Lebanese Muslim strain. Almustafa, the eponymous *Prophet* of Gibran's most famous work, is both a Christ figure and the Universal Man of Muslim civilization. The majority of Gibran's writings are a synthesis of the teachings of these two great religions. His work represents the literary and philosophical meeting-point between the two, as Lebanon provides the social and geographical conjunction. Any true understanding of Gibran therefore depends upon a thorough appreciation of the mutually enriching interchange of cultural and artistic influences for which Lebanon is the traditional arena.

Gibran formed a number of profound and lasting friendships during his life, and none of them was invested with more intensity and spiritual affinity than the relationship he formed through his correspondence with

May Ziadah, a Lebanese writer living in Egypt. For him she *was* Lebanon, and his longing for her and for his country were one and the same thing. 'My longing for my homeland almost destroys me',[5] he wrote to her in 1919, and two years later: 'Are you going alone to our Lebanon? Oh, when will *I* return to Lebanon?'[6] In 1923 he sent her a postcard of Mount Lafayette, New Hampshire, with this message:

Last summer this valley reminded me of the valleys of North Lebanon.
No, no! I have never known a life more pleasant than one spent in valleys. I love the valleys in winter, Mary, when we sit by the fire, with the fragrance of burnt cypress filling the house and the snow falling outside, the wind blowing [it], the ice-lamps hanging outside the window-panes, and the distant sound of the river and the voice of the white storm uniting in our ears.[7]

A few months before his death, Gibran wrote to his friend Felix Farris: 'I wish to go back to Lebanon and remain there forever.'[8] His wish was fulfilled only in death. His body was shipped back to Beirut and buried in the crypt of the Chapel of Mar Sarkis near his birthplace of Bisharri, in August 1931. This chapel has become a national monument to Lebanon's great poet, a permanent reminder of the ideals for which Lebanon stands and which Gibran held so dear.

In a piece entitled 'The Poet's Voice' Gibran wrote:

I am kindled when I remember the place of my birth, and I lean in longing toward the house wherein I grew. . .
I love the place of my birth with some of the love for my land;
I love my country with a little of my love for the world, my homeland;
I love the world with my all, for it is the pastureland of Man, the spirit of divinity on earth.[9]

Gibran's call for unity and brotherhood, his belief in the inevitability of the natural organic process, and his awareness of the necessity of continuity, all of which developed from his appreciation of the distinctive features of his homeland and its history, retain their potency today as do the messages of all great poets.

In today's strife-torn world there is an increasingly urgent need for the voice of Gibran to be heard.

The wise man walks in our midst bearing his heavy yoke; yet is it softer than the breath of a flower and gentler than the breezes of Lebanon.[10]

His friend Mikhail Naimy suggested that Gibran's soul was drawn to the world as a healing agent, as if 'the all-seeing eye perceived our spiritual drought and sent us this rain-bearing cloud to drizzle some relief to our parching souls'[11]

I hope that this book will serve to remind us of Gibran's mission, which is synonymous with that of Lebanon among the peoples of the world. And let no one imagine that the violent image of Lebanon projected in the media is the real one. Today the country is undeniably the victim of international forces, influences and policies, which have turned it into a surrogate battlefield. But the true image and conscience of Lebanon may be found in the works of Gibran. In his paintings and drawings, as much as in his writings, he continually affirmed the principles of universal love, of true fraternity, of unity, and of peaceful co-existence, all of which he regarded as essential to the foundation of a new world order.

I.   HIS LIFE

Family background and early years

On 6 January 1883 near the Holy Cedar Grove on the edge of the Wadi Qadisha (the Sacred Valley) in the small Lebanese town of Bisharri, a son was born to Khalil and Kamileh Gibran. They christened him Gibran Khalil Gibran; today we know him better as Kahlil Gibran.

His father Khalil, whose name the child inherited as his middle name according to Arabic custom, was a tax collector in Bisharri. He is said to have been a heavy drinker and a gambler, with little inclination to shoulder the responsibility of bringing up a family. Years later the poet recalled that his father 'had an imperious temper, and was not a loving person'.[12]

His mother, on the other hand, always meant a great deal to Gibran. Kamileh was the daughter of a Maronite clergyman named Istiphan Rahmeh, and had at first married one of her own clan, her cousin, Hanna 'Abd-es Salaam Rahmeh. Having abandoned her to seek his fortune in Brazil, her first husband then died, leaving her with a young son, Boutros (or Peter). The young widow then married again, this time to Khalil Gibran, the poet's father. After the birth of their son, Khalil, two daughters were born to the Gibrans: Marianna in 1885, and Sultanah in 1887.

Life in Bisharri was hard but not unendurable, and the young Gibran appears to have enjoyed a fairly normal early childhood. He had no formal education for the first twelve

19

years of his life, although he was taught a certain amount by a man named Selim Dahir. The Gibrans lived in a modest house, and the father owned a small plot of land which yielded vegetables enough to feed a family of six. But the father frittered away what income he derived from his work as a tax-gatherer, and the family was obliged to move to one floor of a house whose owner they paid in political allegiance rather than rent. Times were hard, and many Lebanese were emigrating to America, a course which was taken by the Gibran family, with the exception of the father, in the summer of 1895.[13]

Barely twelve years old when he left his native land for the first time, Gibran was to remain deeply attached to the countryside around Bisharri. His mature poetry not only gives a vivid record of that landscape of cedars and streams and waterfalls, but again and again returns to it as the source and symbol of his deepest spiritual longings. For most of his life an exile from his native Lebanon, Gibran continually expressed his wish to return there, impossible though this was in practical terms.

The new immigrants to America settled in Boston's Chinatown among a community of other expatriate Lebanese. Kamileh worked as a seamstress, and also sold various cloth stuffs in the wealthier districts of the city. From the money they earned, the family was able to open a dry goods store, which was run by Boutros with the help of his two sisters. Gibran, meanwhile, was attending the local public school, the Quincy School in Tyler Street. Here his full name, Gibran Khalil Gibran, was changed to Kahlil Gibran, the spelling of 'Khalil' being rearranged to suit the American pronunciation.

The young Kahlil's talent for drawing had already caught his teacher's eye, and he was sent to drawing classes at Denison House, one of several 'settlement houses' which had recently been converted to cater for children in immigrant areas. It was here that his talent attracted Fred Holland Day, the avant-garde photographer. Day encouraged Kahlil to make some designs for book covers, and also used him as a photographic model. Through his association with Day, Gibran gained access to the literary and cultural salons of the affluent Back Bay district of Boston. Here he met artists and writers such as the painter Lilla Cabot Perry; the poet and academic Louise Gurney; and Josephine Peabody, a young and beautiful writer who later proved a benign and inspirational influence on the young Gibran.

In 1898 his family decided to send him back to Lebanon to continue his studies. He returned home and began attending the Al-Hikmah (La Sagesse) School in Beirut. He pursued a course of his own choosing, which contained an important ingredient in terms of his later writing: Arabic literature. This enthralled him, and he familiarised himself not only with ancient and modern works, but also with contemporary literary movements in the Arab world. At the same time, he was absorbing the folklore and colloquial language of Lebanon as revealed to him by his old mentor Selim Dahir. He also began to be interested in French Romantic literature. Soon he was bursting to express himself in words as he had already done with images, and in his final year he was chosen 'poet laureate' of Al-Hikmah School.

By now Kahlil was showing his own characteristic qualities: a lonely intensity, sometimes called sadness; and a fearlessness and outspokeness that he would soon turn to trenchant effect. In Bisharri he fell in love with a local girl, Hala Dahir. Her parents disapproved of Gibran, and the episode resulted in frustration and disappointment for him. It may have been this youthful incident that provided the substance of his semi-autobiographical novella written thirteen years later: *The Broken Wings*, a tale of tragic love, anguish and separation.

When not at school, Kahlil stayed with his father, but the elder Gibran's company cannot have been very congenial to him, and separation from his family in the

United States made him restless. He returned there in 1902, by way of Paris, and, although he was to revisit his homeland briefly when acting as guide and interpreter to an American family, he had now effectively left Lebanon for good. On his way back to America he heard that his sister Sultanah had died of tuberculosis. He hurried home to Boston, only to see Boutros die from the same disease, and then his mother from cancer. Within the space of fourteen months he had lost his younger sister, mother and half-brother. Henceforth he remained with his surviving sister, Marianna. Kahlil had taken over the management of Boutros's store when the latter was confined to bed, but, being ill-equipped for this kind of work, sold the store soon after his death.

At about this time the young Gibran became involved in a relationship with Josephine Peabody that transcended the bond of close friendship. He had joined her 'salon set'[14] and, although at first in awe of her brilliance and beauty, he was soon able to express himself to her on equal terms. Both were defiantly independent characters, passionate about literature and in search of spiritual as well as physical companionship. Josephine called herself Kahlil's muse, and indeed it was she who initially accorded him the title of 'The Prophet'. Perhaps it was to her that Gibran was indebted for the title of his most successful work, which was to be published some twenty years later.

At the height of their relationship Josephine wrote of Gibran:

And to this child of God chiefly my gratitude is due because to him my Soul is no poor foreigner, without the franchise. The gifts it holds out wistfully, expecting not to be heard, he takes with joy, and to him they are substance, richness, gifts indeed. Out of its wishing hands he takes thought, joy, and fullness; and it stands regarding him hearing his thanks – and for all set free – a glorious and liberated life. God bless him that he takes of me my gifts that I would give.[15]

She did him the unique favour of allowing him to peruse

her private journal, and she also arranged for a small exhibition of his works to be held at the nearby Wellesley College. Yet, for all this, Josephine's ardour was the first to cool, and eventually she parted from Gibran. Their contact ended altogether when she married in 1906.

However, this was not before a friend of hers, Mary Elizabeth Haskell, a headmistress from Boston, had made his acquaintance. She visited an exhibition of Gibran's work sponsored by Fred Holland Day at his Harcourt Buildings studio in Boston in 1904. The exhibition was not a commercial success, but Mary Haskell, recognizing the young artist's talent, offered to sponsor another exhibition of his work at her private school in Marlborough Street, and although this was no more successful than the first exhibition, the seeds of a lifelong friendship and collaboration had been sown.

Kahlil Gibran and Mary Haskell

Late in 1904 a fire gutted Fred Holland Day's studio. Gibran's entire portfolio was destroyed, but this unfortunate event had a felicitous outcome; Mary Haskell wrote a letter of commiseration to Gibran, and so initiated a remarkable correspondence between them. It was not until 1907 that their friendship began to blossom, the bond between them being consolidated by their letters. Eventually, early in 1908, Mary offered to pay for Gibran to go on a visit to France and study painting in Paris. Gibran accepted gratefully, and in the few hectic months before his departure they had a chance to become thoroughly acquainted.

On 14 May 1908 they collaborated for the first time on a literary venture – the translation of an Arabic poem.[16] This inaugurated a literary partnership in which Mary's contribution was invaluable to Gibran, and when, five years later, he took the important decision to write in English, she drew closer to him, giving him advice about language whenever he needed it. Almost all Gibran's English works were edited and corrected by Mary before publication. Of their work on *The Madman*, for instance, she wrote: 'He gave always every idea and I simply found the phrases sometimes.'[17]

The spiritual bond between Gibran and Mary endured for well over twenty years. Not long before their friendship formed, Mary had lost an old friend and colleague who had been

24

almost a spiritual guide to her. This loss caused Mary to cut back on her public activities and commitments, and left her in a state of depression. The relationship with the young artist and poet therefore helped Mary as much as it helped Gibran. She received his warm gratitude and love, and came into contact with a spiritual world she would not have known without him. For his part, Gibran received tremendous encouragement and boosts to his morale from her, not to speak of unwavering financial support without which he could scarcely have survived. Mary, realizing that Gibran was by far the most talented of her protegés, began to record every aspect of his life in her journal. She also encouraged him to read English poetry aloud to her and so improve his elocution.

Partly from the deep gratitude he felt towards her, Gibran proposed marriage to Mary in December 1910. She refused him at first, saying 'age made it out of the question'.[18] She also felt it would be a pity 'to spoil a good friendship for a poor love-affair'.[19] Nevertheless, she was in love with him, and 'told him yes'.[20] However, because of the difference in their ages (she was ten years his senior) she stipulated that they should wait two years, and this waiting period, together with some minor matters that Gibran took as injuries, tested their relationship. She finally decided that she could not be his wife, and on 14 April 1911 she recorded her unselfish motives in her journal:

My age is simply the barrier raised between us and the blunder of our marrying. Not my age constitutes the objection – but the fact that for Kahlil there waits a different love from that he bears me – an apocalypse of love – and that shall be his marriage.[21]

After telling him her courageous decision she recorded with immense relief in her journal that 'it has not parted us   it has brought us even much closer together'.[22] Her assessment of the situation was undoubtedly wise, for she became his 'concord soul' without having to marry him. And Gibran was able to tell her in 1922: 'The relation between you and me is the most beautiful thing in my life. It is the most wonderful that I have known in my life. It is eternal.'[23]

Indeed, their relationship weathered all disagreements and difficulties, including financial problems. In 1911 they established their financial arrangements on a new footing. A lump sum from Mary took the place of monthly instalments, whilst Gibran made a will bequeathing many of his personal effects, including all his art work, to Mary. In February 1913, when Gibran moved to his final lodging at 51 West Tenth Street, the question of his finances was brought up again. He and Mary agreed that all previous debts should be cancelled and that she would give $1000 in return for ten representative paintings, to be known as the 'Haskell-Gibran Collection'.[24] The transfer of some securities to his account would complete the package. This financial dependence on Mary certainly must have put some strain on the spontaneity of his feelings towards her.

Late in 1913 a chance remark of hers caused Gibran to give violent expression to his pent-up doubts:

Just tell me what really was your idea in giving me the money, and I shall know where I stand. Tell me simply so that I shall not make a mistake. Was it a gift? Was it a loan? Was it meant to make a bond between us? Tell me. Whatever your intention was, whatever your attitude is, I will try to meet it. But I can't stand the uncertainty. It has been one of the hardest things of my life. . . Months at a time I have suffered terribly from it.[25]

Nevertheless, their relationship withstood such storms. Mary followed the events and relationships in Gibran's life at a distance but viewed them with a fine perception. She understood his sensitivities better than any of his other friends, and was able to give an accurate perspective on these in her journal.

It was in 1922 that Mary told Gibran she had decided to accept the marriage proposal of 69-year-old Jacob Florance Minis. Gibran and Mary reviewed the history of their relationship and made their present position clear; Gibran told her he would love her to eternity, reaffirmed that their union was spiritual, and insisted that it 'would not be changed if you should marry seven times over, to seven other men'.[26]

The marriage took place in 1926, and it inevitably weakened Mary's association with Gibran, especially since her new husband disapproved of the relationship. She brought her journal to an end in 1924, and turned her attention now to her family circle. However, she did not abandon Gibran, for she came to his aid over a faulty investment he had made independently of her with a friend. Mary generously declared that it was merely a mistake, 'and money loss leaves the soul intact after all. . . I've nothing to forgive – nothing'.[27]

She continued to read his work before and after publication, and it is widely held that she provided him with the inspiration for Almitra, the female friend of Almustafa, in *The Prophet*. On Gibran's death in 1931, Mary travelled to Boston, attended the temporary placing of his casket in the vault of the Church of Our Lady of the Cedars, and discovered her letters to him in his studio afterwards. She was the beneficiary of all his art work and the contents of his studio.

Mary Haskell died at the age of ninety in 1964. Her relationship with Kahlil Gibran has accorded her a just immortality, for without her generous patronage Gibran's career would have been very different.

Early career in Boston, Paris and New York

In 1904, having taken the first steps on the road to a career as a painter, Gibran set about ensuring that he maintained at least equal progress in his writing. He decided to relinquish immediate plans for writing in English, a language with which he was as yet not fully conversant. He turned his attention instead to a potential Arab audience of some 20,000 immigrants to America, and beyond them to the Arab world at large. Not long after meeting Mary, Gibran was introduced to Ameen Guraieb, the editor of a New York Arab emigré newspaper called *Al-Mohajer* (*The Emigrant*). Guraieb offered him two dollars a week for a series of Arabic essays. His first published piece in this newspaper appeared under the title of 'Vision'. He did not have a full command of the Arabic language, but his simple style, based on the colloquial peasant speech familiar to him from his childhood in Bisharri, met with the hearty approval of the Arab immigrants, many of whom experienced similar linguistic problems.

Gibran published his first book in 1905. It was entitled *Al-Musiqah* (*Music*), and is a lyrical eulogy of the art of music, very probably inspired by the concerts of the Boston Symphony Orchestra to which he had been introduced by Fred Holland Day. In the following year, the much lengthier work *'Ara'is al-Muruj* (*Nymphs of the Valley*) received publication; a collection of three stories set in Lebanon, it contains attacks on Church and State.

The criticisms of the church, in particular, were renewed with the publication in 1908 of *Al-Arwah al-Mutamarridah (Spirits Rebellious)*,[28] a collection of four prose poems in Arabic. The book contained a self-portrait of the author and an introduction by Ameen Guraieb. The stories represent a plea for the spirit of Liberty, and a condemnation of hypocrisy and evil. Certain Syrian church leaders took offence and had them banned by the Government.[29] Gibran seems to have regarded the adverse criticism heaped on *Al-Arwah al-Mutamarridah* as a compliment; in later years he not only remained undismayed but learned to launch vigorous counter-attacks on his critics.

During this same year of 1908, Gibran's personal relationships were enriched by the acquaintance of two other protegées of Mary Haskell. Both were young women: Charlotte Teller, another writer, who became something of a rival to Gibran for Mary's sponsorship, although her friendship later proved useful; and Emilie Michel, a beautiful French woman who taught at Mary's school and intended to become an actress. 'Micheline', as she was known to her friends, entered into a short-lived love affair with Gibran, apparently with Mary's approval and possibly even with her encouragement. This cooled to a 'solicitous friendship'[30] two years later, and Micheline eventually married in 1914.

The outstanding event of 1908 for Gibran was the start of a two-year stay in Paris, financed by Mary Haskell. He sailed from New York at the beginning of July, and made his way to Paris via London. Mary went to see him in Paris a little later, and Micheline also travelled there to visit her parents, soon discovering that Gibran had found living quarters close by in the Avenue du Maine, Montparnasse.[31] He began studying at the École des Beaux Arts, and at the Académie Julien, which enjoyed a certain vogue among Bostonians at the time. It was here that he encountered a former school friend from Al-Hikmah, Yusuf al-Huwayik. They both found that they had more sympathy with Classicism than with Cubism, which was then flourishing in Paris, and they were both unimpressed by the art of Maître Lawrence, their teacher, whom they soon left in order to work on their own in the autumn of 1909.

Earlier that same year Gibran had turned to a painter whose conception of art appealed to him, the visionary Béronneau. Working without tuition, Gibran and Huwayik shared costs for models, and regularly visited the art galleries and museums together. Though not converted either to Cubism or to Fauvism, Gibran did make some attempt to understand these movements. Some years later he expressed an appreciation of similar works of modern art at an international exhibition in Boston, in a letter to Mary: 'The pictures, individually, are not great; in fact, few are beautiful. But the spirit of the exhibition as a whole is both beautiful and great . . . the spirit of the movement will never pass away, for it is as real as the human hunger for freedom.'[32]

Gibran's true artistic affiliation was with an earlier generation of French painters, the Symbolists Eugéne Carrière, Puvis de Chavannes and Gustave Moreau. He also liked William Turner's brilliant, impressionistic paintings, which he had seen in London.

His own work did not go without recognition. In the spring of 1910 his painting 'Autumn' was shown at an exhibition held by the Societé Nationale des Beaux-Arts, and later the same year he received an invitation from the Union Internationale des Beaux-Arts to contribute six paintings to its autumn exhibition.

One of the highlights of this Paris sojourn was a meeting with the great French sculptor, Auguste Rodin, who subsequently had an important influence on Gibran's work. Rodin spoke to Gibran only briefly, recognizing him from a seminar for art students which he had held in his studio. The impression he left on the young Gibran was considerable.[33] At his studio Rodin talked about William Blake, 'a distinguished poet in his art, and a distinguished artist in his poetry' who 'was not mad, but was a sane man in a company of madmen'.[34] The image of the madman who is in fact the only sane person in his society attracted Gibran to the end of his life. It is no coincidence that the two names most frequently linked with Gibran are Rodin and Blake, though it is possible that Gibran himself dreamed up the often repeated description of himself, accredited to the French sculptor, as 'the William Blake of the twentieth century'.[35]

Gibran retained his contacts with the literary world throughout this period, and continued his contributions to *Al-Mohajer*. *Al-Arwah al-Mutamarridah* continued to attract attention, while a French translation of one of the stories in *'Ara'is al-Muruj* was included in a French anthology of modern novellas. Gibran read widely in European literature – including the Romantics, Rousseau and Voltaire, according to Huwayik[36] – and paid particular attention to contemporary English and French writers. But the work of Friedrich Nietzsche proved to be the strongest influence on Gibran at this time. He read *Thus Spake Zarathustra*, probably in French translation, and immediately fell under the spell of the German philosopher.[37]

In 1909 Gibran received news that his father had died, and this caused him to 'weep bitterly' in spite of the gulf that had existed between them. 'His friends wrote saying that he blessed me before the end came',[38] he told Mary in a letter dated 23 June.

Before leaving Paris in 1910, Gibran met the Lebanese writer and poet Ameen Rihani. Having similar interests they soon became friends, and travelled to London together with their compatriot, Yusuf al-Huwayik. There the three Lebanese laid plans for nothing less than the cultural renaissance of the Arab world. The cornerstone of their programme was reconciliation, especially between Christian and Muslim Arabs, on which depended the future of the entire Middle East. They were particularly concerned about the many hostile factions at whose senseless animosity and warring Gibran had pointed the finger in *Al-Arwah al-Mutamarridah*. Religious fanaticism was their greatest obstacle.

Gibran and his companions were optimistic enough to draw up a rough plan for a Beirut opera house, the outstanding architectural feature of which was to be two domes symbolising the reconciliation of Christianity and Islam. Although the plans never materialised, the proposed opera house was a manifestation of a deeper, more essential aspect of Gibran's identity as an artist and an Arab, an aspect which his mature writings would display more fully: his belief in the need to merge the Sufi Muslim tradition with the Christian mystical heritage of his background. Half church, half mosque, the opera house sketch was intended to represent the marriage of the essential values of the two world religions in a harmonious and unified whole, where each constituent complements and balances the other, drawing on a shared Arab mystic heritage.

Back in Boston, Gibran attempted to give his Arab loyalties semi-political expression. In 1911, following a period of intense political activity in the Middle East, during which time many Arab territories were at last freed from oppressive Ottoman rule, Gibran founded 'the Golden Circle' (Al-Halqa al-Dhahabiyyah). It was one of many semi-political societies which sprang up at that time in France and the United States, as well as in Syria, Lebanon and Turkey. The aim of the Boston group was to combat Ottoman oppression, but it broke up within a few months, apparently because of strong differences over the programme to be adopted. Gibran's visionary belief that it was possible to be morally free whilst languishing in chains was not the sort of solution that appealed to the other Arab emigrants.

On returning to Boston from Paris, Gibran had found accommodation for his sister Marianna and himself at 18 West Cedar Street. Unfortunately the arrangement was not successful; Marianna missed the Syrian community in which they had lived before, and Gibran found his sister's single-minded devotion to him rather overpowering. He was also becoming restless in Boston, feeling it was no longer an artistic centre, and after Mary's refusal of his marriage proposal he moved to New York.

Gibran was fortunate enough to have the use of Charlotte Teller's vacant Greenwich Village apartment, and she also provided him with his first contacts in New York. When Charlotte needed her apartment again, Gibran moved into Ameen Rihani's cramped lodgings at a rooming-house on West Ninth Street. His next move, however, was his last: it found him settling into a 'fine, large studio'[39] at 51 West Tenth Street, dubbed 'The Hermitage' by his Syrian friends. This was to be Gibran's home for the remaining eighteen years of his life.

Soon Gibran was earning a reasonable living as a portrait painter, an occupation which was inevitably bringing him into contact wth distinguished men and women. In October 1911 he sketched W. B. Yeats's portrait, and the two men talked for three hours. Gibran felt that the patriot in Yeats was spoiling his work,[40] a problem he could perhaps appreciate from his own experience. Yeats had turned away in middle life from a romantic, other-worldly stance in his crusade for the Irish National Theatre, something which Gibran had no wish to do or perhaps was incapable of doing (causing him to be accused by one critic of lacking a 'true social and cultural responsibility'.[41]) The two met on at least two other occasions, in 1914 and in 1920, but were never more than acquaintances.

Gibran worked on portraits of several other celebrities including Yeats's patroness, Lady Gregory,[42] and the actress Sarah Bernhardt.[43] Among those he sketched, perhaps the most indelible impression was left on him by

the spiritual leader of the Baha'i Faith, 'Abdu'l Baha, who
was on a tour of Europe and America. Gibran was
introduced to him by a friend, Juliet Thompson, one of the
poet's near neighbours on West 10th Street. Although
Gibran was never to espouse the faith of 'Abdu'l Baha, he
was undoubtedly entranced by his personality. 'Abdu'l
Baha told him: 'Those who work with the Spirit work
well. You have the power of Allah in you. . . Prophets and
poets see with the light of God.' Gibran wrote of him to
Mary: 'In his smile there was the mystery of Syria and
Arabia and Persia.'[44] And he later confided to a friend: 'For
the first time I saw form noble enough to be a receptacle
for the Holy Spirit'.[45]

The influence of 'Abdu'l Baha on Gibran has yet to be
fully appraised, but the Baha'i Teacher, already famed
among Christians and Muslims alike in the Near East for
his exposition of the essential truths common to both
Faiths, clearly struck an answering chord with Gibran's
belief in tolerance, understanding and, particularly, the
underlying unity of all religions. Juliet Thompson, who
knew the poet well, recalled:

[Gibran] told me that when he wrote The Son of Man, he
thought of 'Abdu'l-Baha all through. He said that he was going
to write another book with 'Abdu'l-Baha as the center and all the
contemporaries of 'Abdu'l-Baha speaking. He died before he
wrote it. He told me definitely that The Son of Man was
influenced by 'Abdu'l-Baha.[46]

A few weeks before meeting 'Abdu'l Baha, Gibran finally
published Al-Ajnihah al-Mutakassirah (The Broken
Wings),[47] the Arabic novella on which he had been
working since his return from Lebanon in 1903. The
central theme of the book, which is probably semi-
autobiographical (see p. 21), was once again the corrupting
effects of power. In 1913 he began contributing to Al-
Funoon (The Arts), edited by Naseeb 'Arida, the first
attempt at an exclusively literary and artistic magazine by
the Arab immigrant community in New York. Although
moderately successful to begin with, publication became

intermittent before the magazine folded in 1918. In 1914 some of Gibran's best contributions to various Arab publications were collected and published in book form under the title of *Kitab Dam'ah wa Ibtisamah (A Tear and a Smile).*[48]

Gibran was beginning to experience the divisions created by the pull of fame on the one hand and the demands of his spiritual life on the other. Part of the difficulty was the image others had formed of him, which he did nothing to clarify, but which his wise friend Mary Haskell plainly saw to be the source of unfortunate misconceptions. 'Rihani, Madame [Marie] El-Khoury, Charlotte, Micheline, all consider him a man of "affairs",' she wrote. 'He doesn't undeceive them – simply because he shrinks more from talking about his intimate concerns than from being misconceived.'[49] Elsewhere in her journal she mentions Gibran's embarrassment at being courted by women who professed an interest in his art but in reality sought only to encourage sexual advances from him.[50] Both Mary and Charlotte Teller – who briefly became emotionally involved with Rihani – noted a change in Gibran's personality around 1914. He had grown more able to accept the ambiguity of good and evil in the world, and had become more confident and mature.

Maturity

On the publication of *The Broken Wings* in 1912, Gibran received a letter from a young Lebanese woman living in Cairo. She was May Ziadah, three years Gibran's junior and a writer of literary reviews. This occupation had led her to take an interest in her compatriot's work, and her praise of his Arabic novella was enhanced by a knowledge of his earlier writings. From a correspondence based on mutual interests and admiration, a true love-bond was established, despite the fact that the two never met in person. May was to become perhaps the foremost female literary figure writing in Arabic in the early decades of the century, known and admired by the leading figures of the time who frequented her literary 'salon' in Cairo. May also collaborated with Huda Sha'rawi, the Egyptian suffragette, and remained a lifelong champion of women's rights.

In May Ziadah, Gibran found a person who shared his own spiritual longings. Though he also wrote passionately to Mary Haskell and shared an emotional bond with her, with May Ziadah there was the important factor of being able to express himself fully in his native Arabic. He could write of his homeland with longing and nostalgia and be completely understood. When he wrote to her of his love, he could express it in terms very close to those which a Sufi would use in striving towards the realization of his 'God Self'. Indeed, Gibran and May were lovers of the 'Blue Flame' used by Gibran to symbolise the divine nature within man as well as his eternal love for May.[51]

In 1913 Gibran began to write seriously in English, with the help of Mary Haskell. His first published piece in English appeared in 1915, a poem entitled 'The Perfect World'. It was later included in his first English book, *The Madman* (1918). At this time Gibran seems to have encountered some difficulty in composing his prose-poetry in what was for him a second language. His style was based on the biblical language of the Authorised Version, though his use of the English language always retained an oriental colouring, an Arabic ingredient reflected in both the thought and the phraseology of his writings in this foreign tongue.

Gibran did not allow his increasing involvement in writing to deflect him from continuing with his art. In 1914 a successful exhibition of his paintings was held at the Montross Gallery on Fifth Avenue. Individual paintings were sold for over $1000, and his work made a favourable impression on certain eminent artists in New York, including Albert Pinkham Ryder. This led to further exhibitions in 1917, at the Knoedler Galleries in New York and at the Doll and Richards Galleries in Boston, both featuring a collection of his pen and wash drawings. Gibran's success as an artist reached its zenith with the publication in 1919 of *Twenty Drawings*, with an introduction by Alice Raphael Eckstein.[52] Though her appraisal is couched in hyperbole, it does capture the essential quality of Gibran's art:

It is at [the] dividing line of East and West, of the symbolist and the ideationist, that the work of Kahlil Gibran presents itself as an arresting type in our conception of painting . . . we see a body of a woman who rises out of the vast form of the All-Mother, carrying in her arms man and woman. . . Erda – Amida – Ceres – Mary – the choice is a matter of time and temperament. The meaning is the same and Gibran is dealing with fundamentals. . . His centaurs and horses have a charm beyond their natures so that they are never wholly animal in

character. . . So that, in regarding these centaurs we sense
the beast that is yet man and again the man which is and must
be animal; we become conscious of that evolution upward which
is in itself a miracle, although there is a barrier which will
forever prevent man from clutching the stars.[53]

The Great War had activated Gibran's concern for his
native land, an emotion reflected in his writings at the
time. At heart he was a rebel, but one who had difficulty
in finding the right outlet for his energy. He might have
enlisted and helped liberate his country from the Turks, as
some of his compatriots did, but being physically too frail
for such a venture he decided instead to act as a
mouthpiece for their cause in America. He published an
'Open Letter to Islam', calling on the various native sects
in Ottoman-occupied lands to cease their internecine
struggles and unite in opposition to the Turks, and wrote
other articles deploring the plight of his people and
appealing for aid on their behalf. He also helped organise
a League of Liberation, and was instrumental in the
formation of a Relief Committee which raised funds to
combat the starvation caused by war in the Middle East.

His health deteriorated markedly during this anxious
time, and despite the worthiness of the cause in which he
was engaged he found it hard to cope with the com-
plications involved in dealing with his compatriots. He
told Mary that he was a Syrian and would always remain
so; but although Rihani and the other Syrian immigrants
understood one another, he did not understand them nor
they him. (Gibran used the word 'Syrian' in a regional
rather than political sense; the entire region was under
Ottoman rule, and Syria and Lebanon were treated as one
country for administrative purposes.[54]) This helped him to
realize that 'Syria is not the purpose of my life . . . perhaps
I shall find myself as much an alien there as anywhere
else'.[55]

During these war years the tone of Gibran's writing
changed considerably. His message was no longer one of

hope, but struck a sombre, even nihilistic note. The confident affirmations of love as the ordering principle of life
were replaced by gloomy prophecies of the fall of civilization. In the summer of 1918 he was introduced to Alfred
A. Knopf, a young publisher, who expressed an interest in
The Madman, the work that best illustrates this
pessimistic turn in his thought. Gibran's first book in
English was duly published by Knopf – as were all his sub-
sequent English works – in October of that year, its
appearance coinciding with the end of the war. Its impact
was immediate, and in 1919 Gibran was able to tell May
Ziadah that *The Madman* had been translated into French,
Italian and Russian, and 'parts of it into other languages'.[56]

Further illustration of this darker aspect was provided by
an anthology of Gibran's various journalistic writings in
Arabic, collected from the period 1912–1918 and published
under the title of *Al-'Awasif (The Tempests)*. The theme
of the corruption of civilization is expressed in 'The Grave
Digger', where the chief character, a giant ghost, buries the
hordes of spiritually dead people from a civilized world with
apparent relish. A much shorter and entirely different piece
with the same title appears in *The Madman*.

1919 saw the publication of another Arabic work,
Al-Mawakib (The Procession), a philosophical poem built on
a dialogue between Youth and Age, accompanied by some of
Gibran's best illustrations. Again, through the voice of the old
man representing Age, civilization is seen as an enervating
force, this time bringing disillusionment. The basic literary
device used in *The Madman*, *The Tempests* and *The
Procession* is the parable. In Gibran's hands, whether in Arabic
or in English, this echoes the traditional 'wisdom' stories and
sayings of the East in general, and of the Arab world in
particular. Yet another set of parables is to be found in Gibran's
second English work, *The Forerunner*, published in 1920.

Also in 1920, Gibran became the founder-president of a
literary society known as 'Arrabitah' ('The Pen-bond'),

which was made up of the most distinguished Arab immigrant writers and poets in New York. A forum for discussion about modern Arabic writing, the 'Pen-bond' became an informal club for like-minded writers, with regular meetings at the home of one of its members. Among these was Gibran's compatriot, Mikhail Naimy, whom he first met when working on Al-Funoon in 1916, and who became a close friend and confidant, and later one of Gibran's biographers.

The next three years were spent in thorough revision of the original drafts of Gibran's most successful work, *The Prophet*. During this period he also published two Arabic works: *Iram, Dhat al-'Imad (Iram, City of Lofty Pillars)* (1921), a discourse on mysticism written in dramatic form, and *Al-Badayi' wa'l-Tarayif (Beautiful and Rare Sayings)*[57] (1923), another compilation of Gibran's Arabic writings. The latter work, published in Cairo, included some imaginary pencil-sketches of great Arab philosophers, most of whom had never before been given visual representation.

Another exhibition of Gibran's pen and wash drawings was held in Boston in 1922. His literary and artistic reputation was flourishing, but his health had begun to show further signs of deterioration. The illness, which manifested itself in cardiac pains and nervous debility but was apparently incapable of diagnosis, was to lead to his premature death a decade later. Mary's journal at this time frequently paints a picture of a rapidly aging artist; even as he was working on revisions of his *magnum opus*, he was attending hospital for breathing tests.

Gibran was extremely anxious not to meet his death before the completion of *The Prophet*, which he described as a spiritual pain inside him struggling for expression. 'All that I can say and do is foreign to the real thing that I would say and cannot,' he told Mary in May 1922. 'Only the Prophet has shadow of that thing [sic] – a bit every now and then.'[58] Yet in spite of his ill-health and his struggle for self-expression, Gibran was reaping the benefits of a newly-won fame. He was gaining recognition among a growing number of people, including liberal church congregations whom he was asked to address, and he was enjoying the society of cultured and affluent patrons.

The Prophet – or the 'Counsels', as Gibran and Mary were calling it in 1918[59] – possibly took longer than any of his other works to complete. Gibran once hinted that he originally wrote it in Arabic in his early teens[60], but all the evidence appears to refute this. The first known Arabic version was a translation made from Gibran's English original after his death. His English had improved considerably, and Mary's literary assistance was by now largely confined to matters of spelling, punctuation, and the finer points of grammar. He still maintained that English was a foreign language for him, but Mary recorded in her journal: 'Kahlil's English is the finest I know; it is creative and marvellously simple.'[61] Gibran himself had the following thoughts on the subject, as recorded by Mary:

There are almost no people whose English I kneel before. I have a sense of English and I know many words, for I've an ear for words. It is the shaping of my English expressions that comes slowly to me. English is a fine language. There's nothing that can't be said in it, but one has to use many words. If a thing could be said in ten words, I've tried to say it in three. What was long said, by everyone and in several ways, I've tried to say in a way so perfect that hereafter people would remember only my way. I want to take a common stone, and carve upon it a face that no one can forget.[62]

Gibran considered *The Prophet* to be his best work, and for that reason he refrained from publishing it until he was perfectly satisfied with it, despite the delay which this involved. It finally went on sale in 1923, and all 1300 copies of the first edition were sold within a month. *The Prophet* also contains some remarkable illustrations, including a portrait of Almustafa, described by Mikhail Naimy as 'the loveliest and the most impressive ever drawn by Gibran'.[63]

Mary received her copy shortly before the book became available to the public. Though she had read it many times over in draft and proof form, the final product overwhelmed her, and she wrote to Gibran: 'This book will be held as one of the treasures of English literature. . . Generations will not exhaust it, but instead, generation after generation will find in the book what they would fain be – and it will be better loved as men grow riper and riper.'[64] Coloured by emotion as Mary's judgment may have been, her words contain a fair amount of truth if sales are anything to go by (some three million copies have been sold to date, and only the Bible has sold better in America this century).

Part of the success of The Prophet lies in its title – an inspired choice which, in its equation of poet and prophet, aspires to the highest ideal entertained by Gibran. Yet he was all too aware of the demands of being considered a 'prophet', a title many admirers subsequently accorded him. He told Mary: 'The difference between a prophet and a poet is that the prophet lives what he teaches – and the poet does not. He may write wonderfully of love, and yet not be loving.'[65]

Last Years

After completion and publication of *The Prophet*, Kahlil Gibran had barely more than seven years to live. Yet the exhilaration of unburdening himself had for a moment thrown his illness into the shadows. 'You inquire after my health,' he wrote to May Ziadah in early December 1923, 'and when you do so, my whole being is transformed into a mother full of compassion. I am in the best of health. The ailment I spoke of before has forsaken me, and has left me strong and in good spirits despite the grey streaks it has traced on the hair by my temples!'[66]

As for *The Prophet*, though it had released some of the spiritual energy within him, it was 'only a small part of what I have seen and of what I see every day, a small part only of the many things yearning for expression in the silent hearts of men and in their souls'.[67] The quality of 'aloneness' was a crucial ingredient in the life of Gibran's prophetic figures; it featured in *The Prophet*, and would do so again in his portrayal of Jesus in *Jesus, the Son of Man*. It was also an inbuilt part of Gibran's own nature. As he told May Ziadah:

I am not one of those who belittle the secrets of their souls and what is hidden in their hearts only to publicise them to any wind that blows. It is true that I am a very industrious man; and I yearn for whatever is great, noble, beautiful and pure in just the same way as those others who yearn after greatness, nobility, beauty and purity. But I am also a stranger among men, entirely on my own, just like those other men who are entirely on their

43

own despite possessing seventy thousand friends of both sexes.[68]

Yet 'of all people you are the nearest to my soul, and the nearest to my heart',[69] he assured May.

It has been suggested that Gibran's career reached its peak with *The Prophet*, and that nothing he did subsequently achieved the same heights;[70] indeed, that he had given of himself 'a testimony which is almost perfection in itself'.[71] Gibran was now faced with the inevitable difficulty of providing a sequel. He originally intended *The Prophet* to be the first book of a trilogy, to be followed by 'The Garden of the Prophet', dealing with man's relation to nature, and 'The Death of the Prophet', concerned with man's relation to God.[72] The aim was never achieved, though 'The Garden of the Prophet' was begun and appeared in a posthumous publication with the same title, having been completed by Barbara Young.

With Mary's approaching marriage and the new restrictions it would place on her relationship with Gibran, he needed an immediate source of support, and this was provided by Barbara Young, who became his amanuensis in 1925. She was later to write a hagiographic account of Gibran's life, entitled *This Man from Lebanon* (1945). He found much needed rest and comfort at the homes of patrons, including that of Corinne Roosevelt Robinson, whom he visited every year. He was becoming a celebrity in the English-speaking world following the publication of *The Prophet*, and also in the Arabic-speaking world, where his works went through many editions and his English books appeared in translations by Antonius Bashir. Mary received the pre-publication drafts of his later works at her home in Georgia, but their correspondence eventually dwindled to almost nothing.

His correspondence with May Ziadah continued, however, though not without some difficulties, which were mainly the result of May's diffidence over a relationship that was now based on an open admission of love on both sides. She was evidently constrained by an oriental sense of propriety, and in one of her letters wrote: 'I even blame myself for writing to you, for in writing I find myself taking too much freedom . . . and I am reminded of the words of the venerable men of the East: "It is better that a young woman should neither read nor write".'[73] Gibran continued to send her invitation cards and a variety of post-cards bought in the museums he had visited, as well as unrestrained expressions of his dreams and longings for the East.

In 1925 Gibran was asked to become an officer of the New Orient Society in New York, and to contribute to its quarterly journal, an invitation which honoured him. The editor, Syud Hussein, said of him: 'There is no more sincere and authentic or more highly gifted representative of the East functioning today in the West than Kahlil Gibran.'[74] Apart from 'The Garden of the Prophet' he was also working on two plays in English, 'Lazarus and the Beloved' and 'The Blind'; neither was published at the time, and it was not until 1973 and 1982 respectively that these first appeared in print. In 1926, however, a collection of his aphorisms and proverbs appeared under the title of *Sand and Foam*. Although described by Gibran as a 'stop-gap' work,[75] *Sand and Foam* nevertheless contains a number of memorable sayings, some of which could almost be footnotes to Almustafa's sermons in *The Prophet*.

Recognition of Gibran's achievements took many different forms, and he apparently received an invitation from his homeland to assume political office, for he wrote to Mary late in 1928: 'I told the people of Mount Lebanon that I have no desire to go back and govern them. They wanted me to do that. And you know, Mary, I am homesick. My heart longs for those hills and valleys.'[76]

His long-held desire to return to Lebanon remained unfulfilled until after his death, but meanwhile another of his greatest hopes finally came to fruition: the completion of a book about Christ. Some time after the publication of

Sand and Foam he had told Naimy of his intention to write such a book, partly to refute the popular image of Jesus as a 'sweet lady with a beard':

My Jesus is human like you and me. . . To me he was a man of might and will as he was a man of charity and pity. He was far from being lowly and meek. Lowliness is something I detest; while meekness to me is but a phase of weakness.[77]

Thus it was that Gibran wrote his longest and, some argue, his best work: *Jesus, the Son of Man*, which was published in 1928 with the subtitle 'His words and His deeds as told and recorded by those who knew Him'.

In recognition of Gibran's twenty-five years of service to Arab letters, a dinner was held in his honour by Arrabitah. This took place in New York in January 1929, and glowing tributes were paid him by many distinguished Arab speakers including Philip K. Hitti, who summed up:

The influence which Gibran exercises in modern Arabic literature can be measured, in a way, not only by the multitude of people who have been benefited by reading him but also by the big crop of would-be Gibrans, quasi-Gibrans and Gibran-imitators who have in recent years, mushroom-like, sprung up and flourished all over the Arabic speaking world. So much so that you can hardly nowadays pick up an Arabic newspaper printed in Beirut, Cairo, Baghdad, Sao Paolo or Buenos Aires without finding somebody consciously trying to write Gibran-like. Of course, the esoteric, figurative, imaginative style . . . is not a new thing in Arabic literature. . . But our hero of tonight, through his unmatched mastery of this art, through his pure and rich imagery, through his lofty and noble idealism, through his unexcelled diction and composition – be it in Arabic or in English – has become the father of a new school of thought all of his own. While others use empty words, are affected and artificial, Gibran unfailingly produces gems of thought and is always natural and sublime.[78]

A commemorative anthology, *Al-Sanabil (The Spikes of Grain)*, was also prepared for the occasion.

The following night Gibran was honoured again, this time at the home of the Mexican painter José Clemente Oroczo, and the occasion brought forth readings from many of the works of his youth. Gibran, somewhat weary from the Arrabitah festivities, broke down during the readings and confided to a friend that he wished he could still write as he had done twenty years earlier.[79]

Much more significant than Gibran's mixture of nostalgia and fatigue, however, was the worsening state of his liver. In an effort to subdue the pain caused by his undiagnosed condition, Gibran had been drinking heavily for some time, refusing to see a doctor. In March 1929 he drew up the final version of his will, and wrote philosophically to Naimy: 'My ailment is seated in something much deeper than muscle and bone. I have often wondered if it was not a state of health instead of illness. It is a state, Mischa, whether of health or of illness. . . It is one of the seasons of my life; and in your life and mine there be winters and there be springs; and you and I do not know *in truth* which is the more preferable.'[80] Courageously, he continued working and concealed his condition from most of his friends. He made sure that his sister Marianna would be well provided for, and he also set about purchasing the abandoned monastery of Mar-Sarkees, near Bisharri in Lebanon.

Work on 'The Garden of the Prophet' continued, but Gibran was destined to see only one more of his major works published before his death: *The Earth Gods*, in March 1931. He spent most of his last two years on these two works and *The Wanderer*, which was completed in early 1931 and published posthumously. Of the three, *The Earth Gods*, a dramatic poem begun in 1915, is the most sombre piece. He survived its publication by only two weeks.

On 10 April 1931, at the age of forty-eight, Gibran died in St Vincent's Hospital, New York. An autopsy revealed the cause of death to be cirrhosis of the liver with incipient tuberculosis in one of his lungs. Gibran did not receive a priest on his deathbed, but was accorded a consecrated burial. His body lay in a funeral parlour for a few days so that friends and admirers could pay their last respects. It was then taken to Boston for a funeral service in the Church of Our Lady of the Cedars. The coffin was later shipped to Lebanon and greeted by thousands of his countrymen, who, having heard how his star had risen in the West, had now come to display their admiration. He was buried in his home town of Bisharri. In 1932 his body was moved to Mar-Sarkees, which his relatives had finally succeeded in purchasing. It was the sort of place Gibran must have had in mind when he told Naimy in 1923 that 'the future shall find us in a hermitage on the edge of one of the Lebanon gorges'.[81] Thus had the wanderer returned at last to the home for which he had so long yearned.

II. HIS WORK

Early Arabic Writings

Gibran's writing was characterised from the very beginning by a preoccupation with philosophical matters. His credo as an artist-philosopher was a subjective one, part mystical, part emotional. His youthful work has been described – perhaps unduly harshly – as effusive, sentimental and melodramatic. Yet it is still vigorous and inventive in its choice of subject matter.

Certain beliefs recur in Gibran's youthful work. At this period he portrayed social organisation of every type as evil in that it places the communal above the individual good. Man, however, is seen as essentially innocent, and needs to follow the truth of his own heart only in order to overcome the deadening laws and cruel restrictions of society. Nature, the antithesis of a corrupt civilization, is the best guide. God, or the Universal Soul, is love, and this love is manifest in all Nature. Love is in fact the chief principle of this 'religion of the passions', and offers the sole hope of salvation to unregenerate social man. The souls of the wealthy and the tyrannical are doomed to perdition, whereas the poor and downtrodden have almost achieved the status of prophets.

The chief sacrament of this natural religion is the individual's rediscovery of his spiritual mate and lover, with whom he had been one in God, but from whom he has become separated on entering this world. All unhappiness stems from failing to find one's predestined partner, or from

49

being prevented by society from uniting with him or her. Death offers relief to victims of society and the hope of union to crossed lovers, but only annihilation to the devotees of wealth and power. To initiates of the religion of the passions, death can even be an ecstasy. Reincarnation offers the hope of future recompense for present wrongs, as well as being the process by which man is gradually perfected and assimilated into the Universal Soul.

These ideas were developed by Gibran in the course of his contributions to *Al-Mohajer*. The form he chose was the prose poem, and his themes were presented sometimes in stylised little fables and sometimes in straightforward discourses. His column in *Al-Mohajer*, with the title 'Tears and Laughter', was widely read by the Arab intelligentsia and gained a certain notoriety. The poet proclaimed a message of conciliation and ecumenicism to his country-men, in the same spirit that was later to lead to his collaboration with Ameen Rihani over the Beirut opera house. However, immigration to the New World had unfortunately brought with it the old factional strife among his compatriots that had operated in the homeland. To Gibran, division and plurality were malign attributes of civilization, whereas in the natural world all were united by love. His message for Lebanon, concerning the unity of religion and the oneness of understanding, remained Gibran's prime wish for his country throughout his life.

The combination of Gibran's Rousseau-like belief in the goodness of man when unshackled from the chains of custom and society, and his always-personalised interpretation of the Christian message of universal love, led him to launch a radical assault of Church and State in the two works *'Ara'is al-Muruj (Nymphs of the Valley)* (1906) and *Al-Arwah al-Mutamarridah (Spirits Rebellious)* (1908). But Gibran did not attempt to offer a practical solution to the evils he attacked in *Nymphs of the Valley*; he simply condemned them and advocated a peaceful resignation in the face of hardship. The themes and tone of the work were far removed from the attitudes common among the traditional Arab writers of the day – so much so that they earned him the reputation of being a rebel and a revolutionary.

Gibran's severe criticisms of the church in *Spirits Rebellious* have still not been entirely forgiven; not surprisingly, given such vitriolic denunciations of the priest as 'a betrayer to whom the followers of Christ gave a holy book that he made a net to catch that which belongs to them', as 'a hypocrite whom the faithful girded with a fine crucifix, which he held aloft above their heads as a sharp sword', and as 'a glutton who reveres the well-laden table more than the altar'.[82] The work deals with the same themes as *Nymphs of the Valley*, but in a still more defiant tone. In *Spirits Rebellious*, however, there is some attempt to offer positive alternatives to the evils and abuses so graphically highlighted – even if the solutions are purely Utopian. In the story 'Khalil al-Kafir' (Khalil the Heretic), for instance, the novice Khalil criticises the corrupt behaviour of his fellow monks and is tried for his 'offence' by the village authorities. The villagers rally to his support, and a moral victory is won without bloodshed. Under Khalil's guidance the villagers then gather together and create an Eden-like society.

Gibran took nearly ten years to complete and publish his novella, *Al-Ajnihah al-Mutakassirah (The Broken Wings)*.

It is again concerned with the corrupting effects of power, the story of a young girl who is forced into an unsuitable marriage by her parents. The girl, Selma Karama, suppresses her love for her young lover, and is more or less abandoned by her good-for-nothing husband, dying in childbirth soon after his desertion. The title of the work came from the one-act play *The Wings*, by Gibran's one-time friend Josephine Peabody. Whether or not the novella was actually autobiographical, it would appear to have its origins in Gibran's own unhappy love affair with Hala Dahir in Bisharri in 1899.

Influences and Parallels in the mature works

Kahlil Gibran was an oriental who wrote his most important work in the major language of the Western world. But his mode of thinking and feeling, as well as the form and expression he gave his ideas, is characteristic of the people of the East, and of the Arab in particular. Gibran's constant inspiration was his Arabic cultural and literary heritage; it coloured his English, and it exercised an inescapable hold over his mind. His prose-poetry is both emotive and abstract, based on intuition, and unashamedly idealistic. It lacks the brooding restlessness of a Byron or Goethe, its insistence being upon the wholeness of visionary experience: the perpetual availability of another realm of being besides the mundane, everyday world built on social custom and habit.

Gibran may have been as sceptical about the benefits of civilization as ever were Rousseau or Emerson, but his rebelliousness never extended to challenging the cosmological order or to questioning the nature of divinity itself. He was too steeped in the spiritual acquiescence of the East, and his trust in the reality of timeless, eternal values was too firm to be disturbed even by the pessimism that gripped him in his middle years. Given this frame of mind, it is inevitable that Gibran should have been criticised for his lack of interest in things 'modern', and for his rejection of social life in favour of a mystical, other-worldly order lacking the traits that most obviously characterise modern man.

As a Christian from the Near East, Gibran's native language cannot have been very far removed from the idiom used by Jesus himself. His dearest memories were of a land that had great biblical significance, and it is therefore not surprising that the style of the Bible – particularly its descriptive and rhythmical elements – should have had such a vital influence upon his own style. Almost equally important for him, however, was Islamic culture – above all its Sufi element – which is an inextricable part of Arabic literature and language. Gibran's aphorisms, parables and allegories closely resemble the wisdom of the Sufis. His themes of paradox and illusion, many of which turn on the spiritual blindness or unripeness of ordinary men who are attached to the ephemeral, derive their form and often their content from Sufi literature.

The European Romantics drew much of their inspiration from ideas that filtered indirectly from the East. They in turn inspired Gibran, who merely reinforced his native mysticism with the visionary vocabulary of Blake or Shelley. It is Gibran who, above all others, should be credited with initiating a Romantic School in Arabic literature that was quite distinct from its classical tradition. Through Arrabitah, his influence on other Arab poets acted as a powerful means of conveying Romantic expression – especially enchantment with nature – and bringing about its assimilation into Arabic literature. Gibran adapted Blake and other European Romantics to his own needs because their way of thinking was so akin to his own. In the case of Nietzsche, it was the influence of the form of *Thus Spake Zarathustra* that was most significant, the latter work being, like *The Prophet*, a series of sermons given by an enlightened teacher in response to questions from his audience.

The style of English that Gibran loved best, and aspired to adapt to his own works, was that of the King James Authorized Version of the Bible. The translators had given to the original Hebrew and Greek texts a uniformity of style absent in more literal translations. Gibran's works reveal a specifically New Testament flavour, although the rich imagery and incantational tone of the *Song of Solomon* undoubtedly caught his imagination too. There is a clear echo of the latter in the following passage from *The Prophet*, describing beauty:

> At night the watchmen of the city say, 'Beauty shall rise with the dawn from the east.'
> And at noontide the toilers and the wayfarers say, 'We have seen her leaning over the earth from the windows of the sunset.'
> In winter say the snow-bound, 'She shall come with the spring leaping upon the hills.'
> And in the summer heat the reapers say, 'We have seen her dancing with the autumn leaves, and we saw a drift of snow in her hair.'[83]

Not only a biblical influence is discernible in these lines; their seasonal imagery and even phraseology is strongly reminiscent of Keats's 'Ode to Autumn'. But it is the language of the Gospels that is ever-recurring in Gibran's writing:

> Build of your imaginings a bower in the wilderness ere you build a house within the city walls.
> For even as you have home-comings in your twilight, so has the wanderer in you, the ever distant and alone.[84]

Here the admonitory voice of Jesus can be heard, and he is indeed a primary model for Almustafa, Gibran's prophet. A few lines further on we catch a clear echo of Christ's lamentation over Jerusalem:

> Would that I could gather your houses into my hand, and like a sower scatter them in forest and meadow.
> Would the valleys were your streets, and the green paths your alleys, that you might seek one another through vineyards, and come with the fragrance of the earth in your garments.
> But these things are not yet to be.[85]

There are echoes of other parts of the Gospels, too, especially the parable of the sower. In fact, a large proportion of the teachings of Almustafa is framed in a language very close to that of Jesus in the King James Version:

Oftentimes have I heard you speak of one who commits a wrong as though he were not one of you, but a stranger unto you and an intruder upon your world.

But I say that even as the holy and the righteous cannot rise beyond the highest which is in each one of you,

So the wicked and the weak cannot fall lower than the lowest which is in you also.[86]

The biblical influence on Gibran is so ubiquitous that almost every line he wrote is proof to it, but the metaphorical form he used in many of the didactic stories in his books bespeaks a typically Arabic manner of thinking; for example, the following from *The Madman*:

Said the Eye one day, 'I see beyond these valleys a mountain veiled with blue mist. Is it not beautiful?

The Ear listened, and after listening intently awhile, said, 'But where is any mountain? I do not hear it.'

And the Nose said, 'There is no mountain, I cannot smell it.'

Then the Eye turned the other way, and they all began to talk together about the Eye's strange delusion. And they said, 'Something must be the matter with the Eye.'[87]

Sometimes Gibran's prophet is closer to the Arabian Prophet than to Christ in his words; hence Almustafa's statement on prayer, 'God listens not to your words save when He Himself utters them through your lips',[88] is virtually a rephrasing of a famous saying attributed to Muhammad: 'A servant draws near to me in prayer when I become the eyes with which he sees and the ears with which he hears.' Similarly, in the same discourse on prayer, Almustafa voices thoughts which have evident affinity with Sufi doctrine:

And if you but listen in the stillness of the night you shall hear them saying in silence,

'Our God, who art our winged self, it is thy will in us that willeth.

It is thy desire in us that desireth. . .
Thou art our need; and in giving us more of thyself thou givest
us all.'[89]

Gibran uses wisdom stories — an example of which we
have already seen — in several works from his first English
book, *The Madman*, to his last, *The Wanderer*; and it is in
the 'esoteric, figurative, imaginative style . . . not new in
Arabic literature'[90] that they are written. Such tales should
be seen as Arab meditations recast in the English idiom,
albeit one that is in itself a translation from an oriental
original. It is for these reasons that any ethnocentric
evaluation of Gibran according to the standards of purely
Anglo-American literary tradition is inherently deficient.
He can only be evaluated against an eclectic international
tradition which has not yet been clearly defined — perhaps
an international tradition of the future.

We have already seen the influence of the language of
Keats in an extract from *The Prophet*. But of all the
Romantics it was undoubtedly William Blake who held the
most appeal for Gibran. His influence is apparent in all
aspects of Gibran's work, especially his illustrations. Both
men believed in the poet as prophet, in the existence of the
spiritual worlds, in the precedence of heart over head, and
in 'madness' as the ultimate sanity. Gibran's writings are
filled with echoes of Blake's ideas and expressions, and the
phrase 'A Tear and a Smile', which Gibran used as a title
(in Arabic) for one of his books, seems to have been
inspired by Blake's

> What to others a trifle appears
> Fills me full of smiles or tears.[91]

The sermon on 'Joy and Sorrow' from *The Prophet*,
which contains some of Gibran's best known words, may
have its root in Blake's 'The Mental Traveller'. Thus
Gibran's lines

When you are joyous, look deep into your heart and you shall find
it is only that which has given you sorrow that is giving you joy.

When you are sorrowful look again in your heart, and you shall see that in truth you are weeping for that which has been your delight.[92]

echo Blake's words:

> For there the Babe is born in joy
> That was begotten in dire woe;
> Just as we reap in joy the fruit
> Which we in bitter tears did sow.[93]

Gibran's sense of irony is also akin to Blake's. One example among many may be found in Gibran's tale of 'The Sleep-walkers' in *The Madman*, where a mother and daughter nurture hatred against each other in their sleep, but converse pleasantly upon waking: 'Is that you darling?' . . . 'Yes, dear.'[94] Compare this with Blake's epigram:

> A petty Sneaking Knave I knew –
> O Mr Cr[omek], how do ye do?[95]

The metaphor of the madman or fool, so beloved of Gibran, contains within it a whole world of spiritual paradox which Blake had already explored, especially in the *Songs of Innocence* and *Songs of Experience*, and *The Marriage of Heaven and Hell*. The madman of Gibran's work first realizes he is mad when his mask is stolen by thieves; henceforth he finds joy, freedom and safety in madness, for then 'the sun kissed my own naked face for the first time'.[96] In this state of vision he sees the truth of things, but the people of custom and social habit reject him. This, however, is in itself a testimony to his sanity, for, as Blake wrote:

> 'Madman' I have been call'd: 'Fool'
> they call thee.
> I wonder which they Envy, Thee or Me?[97]

In Gibran's story 'God's Fool', in *The Forerunner*, the dreamer who is a stranger in a foreign land, knowing neither its language nor its customs, takes its sordid behaviour as divine behaviour, and accepts its punishment as an honour. In fact, the fool sees God's image in everything, much like the voice of Blake's poem, 'The Divine Image':

> For Mercy has a human heart,
> Pity a human face,
> And Love, the human form divine,
> And Peace, the human dress.[98]

Gibran's bitter dislike of priests finds its counterpart in Blake's denunciation of the Church in *Songs of Experience*. Further echoes of Blake are found in Gibran's prosody and imagery; for instance, 'When my Sorrow was born', from *The Madman*:

> When my Sorrow was born I nursed it with care, and watched over it with loving tenderness.
> And my Sorrow grew like all living things, strong and beautiful and full of wondrous delights.[99]

is unmistakably reminiscent of Blake's lines describing 'the nurturing of his wrath':

> And I water'd it in fears,
> Night & morning with my tears;
> And I sunned it with smiles,
> And with soft deceitful wiles.
>
> And it grew both day and night
> Till it bore an apple bright. . .[100]

And when Almustafa says:

> Oftentimes in denying yourself pleasure you do but store the desire in the recesses of your being.[101]

Gibran may have been recalling Blake's aphorism in *The Marriage of Heaven and Hell*: 'He who desires but acts not, breeds pestilence.'[102]

Elsewhere in *The Prophet*, Gibran makes use of Blakean imagery, for instance in these lines about clothes:

Some of you say, 'It is the north wind who has woven the clothes we wear.'
And I say, Ay, it was the north wind,
But shame was his loom, and the softening of the sinews was his thread.
And when his work was done he laughed in the forest.[103]

This puts us in mind of Blake's 'Tyger' in its use of personification, and the image of the forest as being the abode of the spiritually awakened:

> . . . & what art
> Could twist the sinews of thy heart?
> . . .
> When the stars threw down their spears,
> And water'd heaven with their tears,
> Did he smile his work to see?
> Did he who made the lamb make thee?
>
> Tyger! Tyger! burning bright
> In the forests of the night. . .[104]

The influence of Blake was clearly paramount, and Gibran made no secret of it. In October 1915 he wrote to Mary Haskell:

Ruskin, Carlyle, and Browning are mere children in the kingdom of the Spirit. They all *talk* too much. Blake is the God-man. His drawings are so far the profoundest things done in English – and his vision, putting aside his drawings and his poems, is the most godly.[105]

From the Romantics as a school, Gibran may have learnt a respect for the divinity of Nature. The following passage from *The Prophet* suggests that the attributes of God are expressed in Nature, a variation on the Romantic vision of Nature as the first revelation of the deity:

Among the hills, when you sit in the cool shade of the white poplars, sharing the peace and serenity of distant fields and meadows – then let your heart say in silence, 'God rests in reason.'

And when the storm comes, and the mighty wind shakes the forest, and thunder and lightning proclaim the majesty of the sky, – then let your heart say in awe, 'God moves in passion.'

And since you are a breath in God's sphere, and a leaf in God's forest, you too should rest in reason and move in passion.[106]

While Gibran was studying art in Paris, he fell under the spell of Friedrich Nietzsche's *Thus Spake Zarathustra* . In fact, all the evidence suggests that this was the only one of Nietzsche's works Gibran ever read. While in Paris he seems to have written two articles on the German philosopher, who remained a potent influence up to the writing of *The Prophet*. Nietzsche's iconoclasm fascinated Gibran. He also liked the German's wit and his fresh, straightforward style. But as a worshipper of beauty Gibran initially believed Nietzsche's philosophy of destruction was all wrong. Then by degrees I found more and more in Nietzsche. Gradually, I came to realize that when we accept a man's form, we also accept his thought.'[107] From Paris, Gibran wrote to a friend:

Yes, Nietzsche is a great giant – and the more you read him the more you will love him. He is perhaps the greatest spirit in modern times, and his work will outlive many of the things which we consider great. Please, p-l-e-a-s-e, read 'Thus Spake Zarathustra' as soon as possible for it is – to me – one of the greatest works of all times.[108]

Apart from *The Prophet*, which undoubtedly owes its sermon-like form to *Thus Spake Zarathustra*, Gibran's other writings contain numerous echoes of Nietzsche. A good example of this pervasive influence is the opening line of *The Forerunner*, 'You are your own forerunner',[109] which clearly recalls Zarathustra's statement, 'Mine own forerunner am I'. But, on Gibran's own testimony, it was the form rather than the philosophy of Nietzsche that he utilized. He also admired Nietzsche's critique of religion, modifying it to his own needs. Nietzsche's attitude towards Christianity – which he hated 'because it stood for softness'[110] – probably aided Gibran in his own efforts to break away from the traditional weak and sentimental picture of Christ when he wrote *Jesus, the Son of Man*. Nietzsche may also have reinforced Gibran's already well-developed distaste for organized religion, and for the hypocritical control he believed it exercised over most of society.

To sum up, the most important influences upon Kahlil Gibran were the Bible, especially the King James Version; Sufi literature in Arabic; the poetry and drawings of William Blake; the sensitivity to nature of the Romantics; and the form of Nietzsche's *Thus Spake Zarathustra*. To these influences might be added the helpful advice of Mary Haskell, which was by no means negligible in the early years when Gibran was struggling with the English language. However, his achievement should not be regarded simply as an amalgam of these various factors, but rather as a visionary literature entirely his own.

Mature works up to the Prophet

Given the importance of *The Prophet* in Gibran's *oeuvre*,
it is not surprising that his works in both Arabic and English
leading up to it have been called exploratory, even rudi-
mentary: the products of 'an extremely sensitive soul grop-
ing its way towards a goal whose contours are yet wrapped
in mist'.[111] But there is another possible view: one that
takes a work like *The Madman* on its own terms, giving
due regard to its trenchant criticism of social values and its
elevation of the outsider-poet-seer. Indeed, *The Madman* has
its admirers, and is perhaps more readily appreciated by those
who are impressed by the tradition of Western pessimistic
literature and thought. The date of *The Madman* is significant in this context; it was published just as the Great War
ended, and represents the deepening pessimism which
characterised Gibran's work at that time.

The work is constructed in a manner that Gibran used
for some of his later pieces, particularly *The Forerunner* and
The Wanderer. It is a collection of parables, the first of them
describing 'how I became a madman':

> One day, long before many gods were born, I woke from a deep
> sleep and found all my masks were stolen, – the seven masks
> I have fashioned and worn in seven lives, – I ran maskless through
> the crowded streets shouting, 'Thieves, thieves, the cursèd
> thieves.'
>
> Men and women laughed at me and some ran to their houses
> in fear of me.

And when I reached the market place, a youth standing on a house-top cried, 'He is a madman.' I looked up to behold him; the sun kissed my own naked face . . . my soul was inflamed with love for the sun, and I wanted my masks no more. And as if in a trance I cried, 'Blessed, blessed are the thieves who stole my masks.'

Thus I became a madman.[112]

Implied here is the doctrine of reincarnation that would figure again in Gibran's work, as well as the notion that ordinary life makes people wear 'masks': in other words, they are untrue to their real selves. Hence the madman is at first frightened and angry when he discovers his masks are gone, but soon blesses the thieves who stole them. Although from this moment on ordinary people laugh at him and fear him, the madman is invested with the power to behold the illusions upon which their lives are built.

In the thirty-four parables that follow, the dominant note is that of mordant irony. Each parable contains a moral, and the subjects covered foreshadow those talked of in the sermons of Almustafa: malevolence, hypocrisy, injustice, conformity, ambition, blindness and puritanism. Sometimes there is poignancy and lyricism, but the sardonic note prevails, as in the tale of 'The Good God and the Evil God', who are continually being mistaken for each other. The madman himself features in several of the parables. One of his attributes is darkness, and he compares himself to the night: 'Yea, we are twin brothers, O, Night; for thou revealest space and I reveal my soul'.[113] Another characteristic is the search of his soul for 'the Greater Sea';[114] he sees other people content merely to remain on the shore, which is symbolic of their limited existence. He is crucified, but not for the sake of anyone other than himself; he also shares loneliness with the mountain and the sea, and experiences sorrow and joy alone. And through all these states there is a note of disillusion, echoed in the final plaint to the 'God of lost souls':

But why should I be here, O God, I a green seed of unfulfilled passion, a mad tempest that seeketh neither east nor west, a bewildered fragment from a burnt planet?

Why am I here, O God of lost souls, thou who art lost amongst the gods?[115]

The Madman evidently applied to the pessimism of its time, for though its garb remained oriental and exotic, its pervading note of disillusion could be understood by anyone who had known at first or second hand the horrors of the epoch just passed. Indeed, May Ziadah thought there was an element of 'cruelty' in it, even of the 'dark caverns'.[116] However, it was not an inopportune work with which to introduce himself to the English-reading public.

Gibran's next two works in Arabic, *Al-'Awasif* (*The Tempests*) and *Al-Mawakib* (*The Procession*), continued the note of pessimism and stressed the corrupting agency of civilization which he had already portrayed in *The Madman*. In the poem-dialogue of *The Procession*, a youth who is a forest-dweller speaks of the unity of life, the non-existence of evil, and the continuation of life in death; in contrast an old man, the representative of civilization, talks with the voice of experience and disillusion.

With the publication of *The Forerunner*, however, Gibran's writing was well on course for the confident mysticism of *The Prophet*. Even the title of the former proved highly appropriate, as this book immediately preceded Gibran's most celebrated work. *The Forerunner*, like *The Madman*, is a collection of parables and apologues, and (with a few exceptions) alternates between stories of kings and princes and debates between different kinds of animals – both common devices in Arab fables.

The doctrine of reincarnation appears once again in the story of the king whose chief enemy, another monarch, dies and is immediately reincarnated in the form of the king's first-born son. Lovers are shown to have been together before birth, and the story of 'The Holy Fool' underlines the purity of the soul that is untrammelled by the trappings of civilization. Earthly power is stripped of its outward show and seen to be dependent on inner illumination; thus, the king who leaves his throne and tells the seeker to find 'him who, though born a king, is without kingdom; and him who though ruled in flesh rules in spirit'.[117] Another king, who imagines himself fit to rule, is humbled by the figure of a naked man who steps out of his mirror and convinces the king of his own spiritual weakness.

The fabular ingredient is also present in those parables in which animals compare their abilities. Their arguments and discussions usually illustrate that the limited notions of truth they entertain are only a small part of reality. Representative of this category is the story of the three frogs, each of whom has an explanation for the movement of the log upon which they are floating downstream. One says the log itself is moving; a second says it is being borne along by the river; and a third says that the sensation of movement is purely subjective. When a fourth asserts that all of them are right, they become angry and push him into the river. Hence the wisest who sees further is punished by his less gifted peers.

Gibran repeated this moral in many of his parables under various guises in order to emphasise the limited apprehension of reality possessed by most men, as distinct from the visionary understanding of the seer-prophet figure. The far-sighted man trusts to the deeper power of the soul, as illustrated in the story of the bird that flies from the Forerunner's heart:

At first it was but like a swallow, then a lark, then an eagle, then as vast as a spring cloud, and then it filled the starry heavens.

Out of my heart a bird flew skyward. And it waxed larger as it flew. Yet it left not my heart.[118]

Here the bird symbolises the power of spirit, and its expansion as far as the heavens recalls the mysticism of the

Hindu *Upanishads* as well as the sayings of the Sufi masters.
The last parable deals with the reception accorded the
Forerunner; initially rejected, he is accepted by the people
only when he addresses them in the language to which they
are accustomed, using the expressions they expect to hear.
He loves his fellow men to excess at the outset, but when
they find fault with his generous attributes he alters his
approach and hides his love beneath a harsh exterior. Only
when he denounces the people do they take him in:

From the housetop I proclaimed you hypocrites, pharisees,
tricksters, false and empty earth-bubbles. . .

It was love lashed by its own self that spoke . . . It was my
hunger for your love that raged from the housetop, while my own
love, kneeling in silence, prayed your forgiveness.

But it is this disguise

. . . that opened your eyes, and my seeming to hate that woke
your hearts.[119]

Yet the work ends with a prophetic vision of a redeemed
mankind, able to accept the prophet in his original love:

Night is over, and we children of night must die when dawn
comes leaping upon the hills; and out of our ashes a mightier love
shall rise. And it shall laugh in the sun, and it shall be deathless.[120]

Thus *The Forerunner* proclaims the certitude of spiritual
advancement, and indeed paves the way for the vision of a
'mightier love' preached in *The Prophet* by Almustafa.

Gibran's insistence on the reality of inner illumination is
also to be found in his Arabic writings of this period, composed
when he was revising *The Prophet*. One passage in particular,
from *Iram, City of Lofty Pillars*, emphasises his concern. The
work is a drama, although it lacks dramatic interest; the
following speech from a character called Amena is
nevertheless impressive:

Time and place are spiritual states, and all that is seen and heard
is spiritual. If you close your eyes you will perceive all things
through the depths of your inner self, and you will see

the world, physical and ethereal, in its intended entirety, and you will acquaint yourself with its necessary laws and precautions, and you will understand the greatness that it possesses beyond its closeness. Yes . . . if you will close your eyes and open your heart and your inner perception you will discover the beginning and the end of existence . . . that beginning which in its turn becomes an ending, and that ending which must surely become a beginning.[121]

The Prophet

The most obvious analogues to Gibran's most celebrated
work are, as already noted, the sayings of Jesus and Nietzsche's *Thus Spake Zarathustra*. The simplicity of Gibran's
language had by now become the most striking feature of
his writing, and this owed much to the New Testament style
which he consciously imitated in his search for the purest
form of expression in which to enshrine his spiritual
message. As for Nietzsche, there are numerous points of
comparison between his work and that of Gibran, the chief
one being the similarity between the two prophets,
Zarathustra and Almustafa. Both are strangers among men
who give of their wisdom and then retire to their distant
island homes. But their respective teachings differ enor-
mously in substance; whereas Zarathustra preaches a
destructive code of self and self-reliance, Almustafa's
message to the people of Orphalese is a passionate belief in
the healing power of universal love and the unity of being,
based on the mystic traditions of the Sufis.

There is a widely held theory that *The Prophet* is partly
autobiographical, Gibran depicting himself as Almustafa,
Mary Haskell as Almitra, Orphalese being America, and
Lebanon the 'isle of his birth'. Mary corroborated this view:
'When he described the Hermit poet of the "Counsels" and
the relation of the people of the City to him, it was a description to the very heart of the way people are towards

68

himself.'[122] Gibran, too, virtually said as much when he was in the process of writing the book: 'In *The Prophet*, I have imprisoned certain ideals, and it is my desire to live those ideals.'[123] He later expanded on this: 'I want some day simply to live what I would say, and talk to people. I want to be a teacher.'[124]

Almustafa preaches altogether twenty-six poetic sermons on a wide range of human subjects, ranging from Love, Joy and Sorrow, Freedom, Good and Evil, to Prayer, Religion and Death. The occasion for these is his final departure from the land of Orphalese, which he leaves with sadness, for he has given the people much of himself. It is Almitra, the seeress, who begs him to 'give us of your truth'.[125] She is aware, too, of his 'longing for the land of your memories and the dwelling place of your greater desires'.[126] Almustafa's departure for 'the isle of his birth' in fact symbolises his return to the unborn state from which, as he promises at the end, he will again be reincarnated: 'A little while, a moment of rest upon the wind, and another woman shall bear me.'[127]

Gibran's Prophet, like Krishna in the Bhagavad Gita, reincarnates not only out of the need for continued self-realization, but also to provide an example for the spiritually uninitiated.

He is solitary among the people, however. In Orphalese he has experienced long 'nights of aloneness', and asks: 'Who can depart from his pain and his aloneness without regret?'[128] But, as Almustafa later explains in his sermon on Joy and Sorrow, such suffering is a prerequisite for true happiness and indeed, in its deepest reality, is indistinguishable from it. Almitra also refers to the Prophet's aloneness: 'In your aloneness you have watched with our days. . .'[129] At the close, Almustafa explains the necessity of this quality:

And some of you have called me aloof, and drunk with my own aloneness . . .

How could I have seen you save from a great height or a great distance?

How can one be indeed near unless he be far?[130]

Almustafa's is not the aloneness that condemns the ordinary people – as is Zarathustra's – but the inherent loneliness of the loving prophet who has no peers. This was a subject on which Gibran could write feelingly, having had personal experience not only of the loneliness of a would-be teacher, but also that of the artist and creator.

Almustafa speaks first on Love, and this is perhaps the most outstandingly beautiful of all his sermons:

Love has no other desire but to fulfil itself.

But if you love and must needs have desires, let these be your desires:

To melt and be like a running brook that sings its melody to the night.

To know the pain of too much tenderness.

To be wounded by your own understanding of love;

And to bleed willingly and joyfully.

To wake at dawn with a winged heart and give thanks for another day of loving;

To rest at the noon hour and meditate love's ecstasy;

To return home at eventide with gratitude;

And then to sleep with a prayer for the beloved in your heart and a song of praise upon your lips.[131]

The concept of love as wounding and painful, even while it can lift to ecstasy, is found in the writings of both the Sufis of the east and the Medieval Christian mystics. Almustafa's insistence on the essential identity of love, joy, pain and sorrow, is a major feature of *The Prophet*, and evidently contained very real personal significance for Gibran. It is also a part of the work's rejection of the limiting dualism of the material world and its recognition that truth never *is*, but is always in the process of *becoming*, always spontaneous, as Schiller perceived:

Truth is not something that can be received from outside, like the actuality or the sensuous existence of things; it is something that the intellectual faculty produces spontaneously, in its freedom. . .[132]

Hence Almustafa's refusal to admit absolute good and bad, and his defence of the guilty as being members of the whole like everyone else: 'The righteous is not innocent of the deeds of the wicked', and 'You cannot separate the just from the unjust and the good from the wicked'.[133]

These statements seem at first to contradict the recorded words of Jesus. Gibran probably saw them as corrective of the crudely dualistic interpretations of Christian righteousness that resulted in the separation of man from man. The point is made without recourse to didacticism, and indeed the gentle tone of *The Prophet* is remarkable for the absence of the controversial element present in the early Arabic works and of the sardonic irony of *The Madman*. In the sermon on Prayer, for example, the condemnation of religious hypocrisy is subtle and implicit:

You pray in your distress and in your need; would that you might pray also in the fullness of your joy and in your days of abundance.[134]

What Gibran had done, in fact, was to distil and express with greater profundity the beliefs of those earlier writings of his, such as the pieces published in *Al-Mohajer*.

The note of compassion is expressed again in the work's view of man, who is seen to be in need of self-realization, a bridge between the 'pygmy' in him and his 'god-self'.[135] Self-knowledge comes through listening in silence to the heart's knowledge. This, however, is always harmed by the attempt to form it in words. Nonetheless, the power of universal love is to be felt in all:

Who among you does not feel that his power to love is boundless?[136]

Compared with this power, evil does not exist; as in

Dante's view, evil is a misdirection of the desire for good, or rather it is merely a limitation of that desire. Gibran might also have agreed with Emerson that even a fallen man is moving toward the greater good:

> You are good when you walk to your goal firmly and with bold steps.
> Yet you are not evil when you go thither limping.
> Even those who limp go not backward.[137]

Beside this transcendentalism is an avowal of immanent divinity that recalls both the Psalms and William Blake:

> And look into space, you shall see Him walking in the cloud, outstretching His arms in the lightning and descending in rain.
> You shall see Him smiling in flowers, then rising and waving His hands in trees.[138]

The secret of *The Prophet's* appeal probably rests, then, in its positive approach and its choice of words of praise rather than of criticism, raising the heart of the reader rather than putting it down. To this must be added an acknowledgement of the work's unique mixture of poetry and insight, humanitarianism and inspiration. *The Prophet* proved to be the quintessence of Gibran's message that purified and enshrined all he had desired to say until then. With the exception, perhaps, of one other work – *Jesus, the Son of Man*, which was written with a slightly different intention – Gibran would not reach the same heights again. Yet for Gibran himself the book represented 'only a small part of what I have seen and of what I see every day, a small part only of the many things yearning for expression in the silent hearts of men and in their souls'.[139]

Last works

There are echoes of Almustafa's words in parts of *Sands and Foam* (1926), the next of Gibran's works to be published, but the predominant influence in this collection of aphorisms is that of William Blake. Some of these aphorisms were translated from Arabic and had already received publication in that language. To Almustafa's sermon on Love could be added: 'Love which is not always springing is always dying',[140] and a variation on the same theme, 'Love that does not renew itself every day becomes a habit and in turn a slavery'.[141] The sermon on Giving in *The Prophet* is almost surpassed by two aphorisms in *Sand and Foam*:

Generosity is not in giving me that which I need more than you do, but it is in giving me that which you need more than I do.[142]

and

Generosity is giving more than you can, and pride in taking less than you need.[143]

Similarly, the following might be added to Almustafa's teaching on Children:

If there is such a thing as sin, some of us commit it backward following our forefathers' footsteps;

And some of us commit it forward by overruling our children.[144]

That Gibran's next work, *Jesus, the Son of Man* (1928), had long been crystallising in his mind is borne out by an earlier prose piece in Arabic entitled 'The Crucified', in which he makes abundantly clear his feelings about Christ:

> The Nazarene was not weak! He was strong and is strong! But the people refuse to heed the true meaning of strength.
>
> Jesus never lived a life of fear, nor did He die suffering or complaining. . . He lived as a leader; He was crucified as a crusader; He died with a heroism that frightened His killers and tormentors.
>
> Jesus was not a bird with broken wings; He was a raging tempest who broke all crooked wings. He feared not His persecutors nor His enemies. He suffered not before His killers. Free and brave and daring He was. He defied all despots and oppressors. He saw the contagious pustules and amputated them. . . He muted Evil and He crushed Falsehood and He choked treachery.[145]

When Gibran did complete his essay on the Messiah it was his longest work. Largely based on the Gospels, it nevertheless employs an original scheme – which has been likened to Browning's method in *The Ring and the Book* – whereby seventy-eight different impressions of Jesus are imaginatively attributed to his contemporaries (hence the subtitle: 'His words and deeds as told and recorded by those who knew Him'), and also to others who are entirely fictional. Gibran's vision of Christ, as it emerges through these imaginary accounts, is poetical and highly unorthodox, with no pretensions to historical accuracy. His Jesus is not born of a virgin, he does not die for our salvation, and he is not resurrected. His miracles are the result of natural phenomena, and he teaches the doctrine of reincarnation.

Even before reading *Jesus the Son of Man* one can surmise Gibran's attitude to Christ from his finely sketched frontispiece to the book; in this portrait Jesus has a powerful head, with steep forehead, heavy eyebrows, a full mouth and strong chin, and a neck that might withstand a guillotine – all quite different from the traditional image. In this way we are prepared for Gibran's portrayal of Jesus in words. Perhaps the most powerful expression of Gibran's conception is placed in the mouth of Nathaniel:

I am sickened and the bowels within me stir and rise when I hear the faint-hearted call Jesus humble and meek, that they may justify their own faint-heartedness; and when the downtrodden, for comfort and companionship, speak of Jesus as a worm shining by their side.

Yea, my heart is sickened by such men. It is the mighty hunter I would preach, and the mountainous spirit unconquerable.[146]

Much of the effectiveness of *Jesus, the Son of Man* lies in Gibran's examination of Christ from the viewpoints of many well-known characters from the Gospels, thus giving a fresh angle on a number of familiar stories. Along with those of the disciples, the Virgin Mary and Mary Magdalen, there are also the views of 'anti-heroes' such as Caiaphas and Pontius Pilate; also of Barabbas, who makes the rueful remark that: 'His crucifixion endured but for an hour. But I shall be crucified unto the end of my years.'[147] It falls to John, the son of Zebedee, to explain Gibran's choice of title:

Now you would know why some of us call Him the Son of Man.

He Himself desired to be called by that name, for He knew the hunger and the thirst of man, and He beheld man seeking after His greater self.

The Son of Man was Christ the Gracious, who would be with us all.

He was Jesus the Nazarene who would lead all his brothers to the Anointed One, even to the Word which was in the beginning with God.

In my heart dwells Jesus of Galilee, the Man above men, the Poet who makes poets of us all, the Spirit who knocks at our door that we may wake and rise and walk out to meet truth naked and unencumbered.[148]

John also places Jesus in the context of other avatars who have walked the earth:

Many times the Christ has come to the world, and He

has walked many lands. And always He has been deemed a stranger and a madman.[149]

This image synthesises a number of ingredients that we have already seen in Gibran's idea of the Prophet. It recalls Krishna's words when he tells Arjuna he has been born many times; it implies acceptance of the depiction of Christ found in the opening chapter of St John; and it repeats the notion of the Prophet as an outsider and a 'madman'.

Elsewhere in the work, Jesus is seen to be aloof, an inhabitant of the mountains and hills, once again having the quality of 'aloneness'. In the first account in the book, James the son of Zebedee recalls Jesus looking down from the summit of Mount Hermon, his face shining 'like molten gold', and saying:

In truth the earth is fair and all that is upon her is fair.[150]

Jesus is seen to be a lord of the landscape about him, a man from the 'North Country' (a reference to Galilee) whose lordly attributes are, as in Nathaniel's description, often evoked by lofty natural images. Thus, in the same account:

Shall a man bold enough to say these things to those who ruled Judea be deemed meek and humble?

Nay. The eagle builds not his nest in the weeping willow. And the lion seeks not his den among the ferns.[151]

Jesus is seen by one contributor – 'a philosopher' – as a visionary who continually experienced the truth of the created world, but with a depth and an intensity beyond human capacity:

His senses were all continually made new, and the world to Him was always a new world.

To Him the lisping of a babe was not less than the cry of all mankind, while to us it is only lisping.

To Him the root of a buttercup was a longing towards God, while to us it is naught but a root.[152]

Nicodemus, the poet, is another who expresses the truth of Christ in natural terms:

But Jesus was not claiming more than the month of May claims in her high tide.

Was he not to tell the shining truth because it was so shining?[153]

To Mary Magdalen, Jesus had both strength and gentleness:

And he was gentle, like a man mindful of his own strength.[154]

More abrasive is the opinion of Mannus the Pompeiian, who writes to a Greek:

And Jesus, the man who revealed God as a being of joy, they tortured Him, and then put Him to death.

These people would not be happy with a god. They know only the gods of their pain.[155]

As in *The Prophet*, Gibran challenged orthodox doctrine, in this case by breathing new life into a story grown stale, perhaps, through age and constant repetition. He also managed to re-focus attention on the joyous side of the Gospels. What is most effectively conveyed in *Jesus, the Son of Man* is the sense of a great natural power, inexorable and revivifying, operating through Jesus; and it is this that gives the book its visionary force. Original and strikingly real, its inspirational intensity perhaps exceeds even that of *The Prophet*. It was to be Gibran's last successful work.

In a letter to Mary Haskell, dated May 1929, Gibran expressed the desire to write a book on Shakespeare,[156] a project which, had it materialised, would surely have produced fascinating results. As it turned out, he did not have time to finish his other major project, the two sequels to *The Prophet* mentioned earlier. *The Garden of the Prophet*, started by Gibran some two years before his death, appeared in 1933, having been completed and edited by Barbara Young. Not surprisingly, it is a somewhat incoherent and unpolished work which repeats Gibran's philosophy rather than enlarging on it. Years earlier he had described his intended scheme to Mary:

He has gone to his island – and there he spends a great deal of his time in his mother's garden. – He has nine disciples, who talk with him in the garden. And he talks to them about how the small things and the great things are connected – of man's kinship with the universe. . . It deals with man's relation to the universe – just as the Prophet dealt with his relation to his fellow men.[157]

Mary also gives an idea of the tone and approach of the projected book:

It's personal, his personal experience and feelings – more lyrical with less wisdom [than *The Prophet*]. He talks to his sister Mist: 'We two shall not part again until you are dew in a garden and I a babe on the breast of a woman.[158]

Gibran did manage to finish his sombre dramatic poem, *The Earth Gods* (1931). The work is concerned with the all-embracing unifying power of love but, more than any of his other works, comes across like a didactic piece dressed in literary finery. The prosody is ponderous, deriving its form from the Romantics but in a laboured manner, as in the following lines, which recall Blake and Yeats:

> Now I will rise and strip me of time and space,
> And I will dance in that field untrodden,
> And the dancer's feet will move with my feet;
> And I will sing in that higher air,
> And a human voice will throb within my voice.[159]

Here the device of repetition, which Gibran had used before to telling effect, merely holds up the verse. The fourth line in particular is an example of the vapid generalising that can so easily beset 'ethereal' poetry.

The interest of *The Earth Gods* lies in the debate that takes place between the First God and the Second God. The former is pessimistic, tired of the unending cycle of life and death:

> Weary is my spirit of all there is.
> I would not move a hand to create a world
> Nor to erase one.

I would not live could I but die,
For the weight of aeons is upon me,
And the ceaseless moan of the seas exhausts my sleep.[160]

The second God, on the other hand, is optimistic, and believes that the life they see below them contains within it the seeds of transcendence. He tells his associate:

We are beyond and we are the Most High
And between us and boundless eternity
Is naught save our unshaped passion
And the motive thereof. . .
Yea, in your own soul your Redeemer lies asleep,
And in sleep sees what your waking eye does not see.[161]

This is the voice of Almustafa, encouraging spiritual quest. But there is a Third God who moderates the debate, and counsels acceptance of their predicament:

We shall pass into the twilight;
Perchance to wake to the dawn of another world.
But love shall stay,
And his finger-marks shall not be erased. . .
Better it is for us, and wiser,
To see a shadowed nook and sleep in our earth divinity,
And let love, human and frail, command the coming day.[162]

Critics have noted a mellowness in these lines that had not hitherto been present in Gibran's writings. The spiritual turbulence of his youthful work and the high aspiration of his early manhood had perhaps been replaced by the resignation of a dying man – for Gibran knew he did not have long to live when he wrote *The Earth Gods*.

There remained one more statement to come from his pen: this was *The Wanderer* (1932),[163] appropriately regarded as Gibran's last work, since *The Garden of the Prophet* was left far from complete by him.

The Wanderer, consisting of fifty-two parables in very much the same style as *The Madman* and *The Forerunner*, crystallises Gibran's peaceful message. The parable entitled 'The River', strongly reminiscent of Longfellow's

Hiawatha, with the river symbolising the course of human life, is eloquent testimony to Gibran's love for his Lebanese homeland:

In the valley of Kadisha where the mighty river flows, two little streams met and spoke to one another:

One stream said: 'How came you, my friend, and how was your path?'

And the other answered, 'My path was most encumbered. The wheel of the mill was broken, and the master farmer who used to conduct me from my channel to his plants, is dead. I struggled down oozing with the filth of those who do naught but sit and bake their laziness in the sun. But how was your path, my brother?'

And the other stream answered and said: 'Mine was a different path. I came down the hills among fragrant flowers and shy willows; men and women drank of me with silvery cups, and little children paddled their rosy feet at my edges, and there was laughter all about me, and there were sweet songs. What a pity that your path was not so happy.'

At that moment the river spoke with a loud voice and said: 'Come in, come in, we are going to the sea. Come in, come in, speak no more. Be with me now. We are going to the sea. Come in, come in, for in me you shall forget your wanderings, sad or gay. Come in, come in. And you and I will forget all our ways when we reach the heart of our mother the sea.[164]

The allegory sums up Gibran's view of life in an open, straightforward manner. Indeed, the imagery is so simple that it could have come straight from a children's story. Effortless, but deeply felt, Gibran's perspicuous prose is the fruit of a lifetime's dedication to perfecting an instrument whereby he could communicate to others, in the most effective and beautiful manner possible, the unseen order which he believed to be at the heart of everything on earth.

*   *   *

A definitive biography of Gibran has yet to be written. The existing critical apparatus of Western literary criticism lacks the relevant criteria by which to judge Gibran, and opinions of his work swing violently from the eulogistic to the condemnatory.[165] What is irrefutable, however, is that *The Prophet* is among the most widely read books of the century, despite first appearing in an age when it was impossible to generate by intensive publicity the kind of sales which modern best-sellers enjoy. *The Prophet* does indeed hold an ambiguous position in the field of English literature, a position which has so far debarred it from serious critical attention in the West. It is neither pure literature, nor pure philosophy, and as an Arab work written in English it belongs exclusively to no particular tradition.

In the intellectual climate created by the generation of Freud, Marx and Darwin, Gibran has remained beyond the pale for most critics, who have found themselves disquieted, disarmed or simply embarrassed by his genre of inspirational writing with its emphasis on spirituality and its flouting of much that they hold sacred. One or two critics, like the Irish poet *AE* and the American poet Robert Hillyer, have suggested the adoption of a new critical mechanism for assessing this type of literature deriving from two separate cultural traditions and bound by the prejudices and restrictions of neither.

But it matters little whether *The Prophet* will ever receive universal critical acclaim. The book's greatest strength is its avoidance of opaque philosophical terminology in favour of a consolatory tone which has already succeeded in inspiring many, touching their lives in countless ways and giving them comfort, hope and joy. Likewise, in his great love for the figure of Christ, Gibran created, in *Jesus, the Son of Man*, a different but vital portrait of the founder of Christianity which has the power to break through many stale images and preconceptions.

Gibran's was a unique consciousness; he cannot easily be judged along with his Arab or American contemporaries. He is one of those rare writers who actually transcend the barrier between East and West, and could justifiably call himself – though a Lebanese and a patriot – a citizen of the world. It was, however, as a man from Lebanon that he spoke, and it was a Lebanese mode of thought and belief he ardently expressed.

Gibran is only one of a long line of writers who were indelibly affected by their origins, and whose works carry that as their most recognizable hallmark. For Thomas Hardy it was the South West of England and its thick overlay of historical association that provided the terrain which he imaginatively reshaped to create the setting for his Wessex novels; the verdant woodlands and sea-drenched valleys of New England, that oasis of rural tranquility in the midst of industrial America, inspired the verse of Robert Frost; and the sands of Sligo Bay, the emerald loughs and rivers of Western Ireland and the legendary mountains of Ben Bulben and Knocknarea gave William Butler Yeats an inexhaustible store of symbol and image with which to fire his poetic imagination. For Gibran the land that provided the lasting inspiration for his work was Lebanon, unique in so many ways, particularly in its geographical position and its admixture of ethnic groups; Lebanon of the sacred cedar grove, of the dreaming ruins of the Temple of Astarte, of the lofty snow-capped mountains soaring into heaven. Much of what he gave to the world he owed to his homeland. Perhaps most of all he was indebted to Lebanon for his awareness of the inestimable blessings that flow from the harmonious coexistence of differing peoples and faiths, as well as his vivid apprehension of the catastrophes that must inevitably result from the breakdown of such coexistence.

He therefore spoke in two voices: a voice of consolation, of hope and survival in the pursuit of peace and unity; and a voice of admonition, of warning, with the threat of dire consequences should mankind ever cease to pursue these goals. In a period of history sometimes characterised as the 'Age of Anxiety' – when anger, disintegration, corruption, disorientation and anarchy were the order of the day – Kahlil Gibran stood on his own, emphasising the importance of reconciling reason and passion, of balancing the physical with the spiritual, of perceiving the divine order that is inherent in all things on earth and in heaven, and conforming to its bidding. Gibran's constancy in proclaiming his views, when similar schools of thought were retreating in disorder before the massed battalions of materialism and existentialism, surely foreshadowed the resilience and fortitude displayed by his countrymen half a century after his death; a people who, in the face of devastating and convulsive upheavals, have stood firm in defence of the values enunciated by Gibran, and, with unflinching resolve, continued to proclaim his message, the message of Lebanon, to an unheeding world.

NOTES

Abbreviations

B.P. = *Beloved Prophet: The Love Letters of Kahlil Gibran and Mary Haskell and her Private Journal*, ed. Virginia Hilu (London, Quartet 1973).

Blue Flame = *Blue Flame: The Love Letters of Kahlil Gibran to May Ziadah*, trans. and ed. S. B. Bushrui and S. H. al-Kuzbari (Burnt Mill, Longman 1983).

J & K Gibran = *Kahlil Gibran: His Life and World*, Jean and Kahlil Gibran (New York Graphic Society 1974).

Naimy, K. G. = *Kahlil Gibran, His Life and His Work*, Mikhail Naimy (Beirut, Khayats 1964).

1. Quoted in *A Poet and His Country: Gibran's Lebanon*, ed. Bushrui et al. (Beirut, Middle East Press Inc., 1970), p. 2.
2. *Kahlil Gibran: A Self-Portrait*, trans. & ed. A. R. Ferris (London, Heinemann 1960), pp. 21–22.
3. Kahlil Gibran, *A Tear and a Smile*, trans. H. M. Nahmad (London, Heinemann 1950), p. 139.
4. Kahlil Gibran, *Jesus, the Son of Man* (London, Heinemann 1954), p. 82.
5. *Blue Flame*, p. 12.
6. *Ibid.*, p. 54.
7. *Ibid.*, p. 74. Gibran used May's name in its variations: May, Mary, Miriam.
8. *Kahlil Gibran: A Self Portrait*, p. 93.
9. *A Tear and a Smile*, pp. 176–7.
10. *Ibid.*, p. 60.
11. Naimy, *K. G.*, p. 264.
12. *B.P.*, p. 32.
13. *Blue Flame*, p. 103. Other authors give the date as 1894. Gibran's birth-date has also been the subject of some confusion, since an Arab editor mistakenly translated 6 January 1883 as 6 December 1883 (see *ibid.*, pp. 45 and 86).
14. J & K Gibran, p. 97.
15. *Ibid.*, p. 120.
16. *Ibid.*, p. 171.
17. Quoted in *Ibid.*, p. 284.

18. *B.P.*, p. 28.
19. *Ibid.*, p. 29.
20. *Ibid.*
21. *Ibid.*, pp. 34–35.
22. *Ibid.*, p. 36.
23. *Ibid.*, p. 391.
24. J & K Gibran, p. 248.
25. *B.P.*, pp. 142–3.
26. *Ibid.*, p. 374.
27. Quoted in J & K Gibran, p. 377.
28. *Spirits Rebellious* and *Nymphs of the Valley* were translated posthumously and first appeared in English, under these titles, in 1948.
29. While this work was going to press, Gibran was working on a piece entitled *Falsafat al-Din wa'l Tadayyun (The Philosophy of Religion and Religiosity)*, which was never published.
30. J & K Gibran, p. 193.
31. *Ibid.*, p. 174.
32. *B.P.*, p. 129.
33. The notice that Rodin took of Gibran has been greatly overstressed. This may have stemmed from Gibran's own recollections, for he certainly met Rodin and sketched him, as he did other prominent Frenchmen including Debussy, Rostand, and the critic Rochefort (J & K Gibran, p. 196.). As a young man Gibran had a tendency to romanticise his background and colour his experiences when talking about himself to others.
34. Naimy, *K. G.*, p. 88.
35. J & K Gibran, p. 328.
36. In his memoirs, edited by Edvique Juriedini Shaybouh, published in Arabic in Beirut, 1957.
37. In a letter to Mary Haskell he claimed to have read Nietzsche in his early teens (*B.P.*, p. 88).
38. *B.P.*, p. 22.
39. *Ibid.*, p. 118.
40. J & K Gibran, p. 219.
41. Khalil S. Hawi, *Kahlil Gibran, His Background, Character and Work* (Beirut, American University of Beirut 1963), p. 280.
42. J & K Gibran, p. 222.
43. *Ibid.*, p. 250.
44. *B.P.*, p. 78.
45. *Vignettes from the Life of Abdul Baha*, coll. & ed. Annamarie Honnold (Oxford, George Ronald 1982), p. 158.
46. Marziah Gail, *Other People, Other Places* (Oxford, George Ronald 1982), p. 228.
47. The work was published by Najeeb Diab, the editor of *Mirat al-Gharb (Mirror of the West)*. The first English version appeared in 1959.

48. The first English version appeared in 1947, under the title *Tears and Laughter*. Another version, under the correct title *A Tear and a Smile*, was published in 1950.
49. Quoted in J & K Gibran, p. 235.
50. *B.P.*, p. 72.
51. *Blue Flame*, p. xv.
52. Eckstein's introduction originally appeared as an article in *The Seven Arts*, a periodical to which Gibran had been a contributor.
53. Kahlil Gibran, *Twenty Drawings*, with an introduction by Alice Raphael (New York, Vintage Books 1974), pp. 9–11.
54. In 1918, after the collapse of the Ottoman empire, both countries were placed under a French mandate. History was finally respected with the granting of independence to Lebanon in 1943 and to Syria in 1946.
55. Quoted in J & K Gibran, p. 291.
56. *Blue Flame*, p. 16.
57. Also known as *Best Things and Masterpieces*.
58. *B.P.*, p. 383.
59. *Ibid.*, p. 303.
60. *Ibid.*, p. 322.
61. *Ibid.*, p. 327.
62. *Ibid.*, p. 341.
63. Naimy, *K. G.*, p. 191.
64. *B.P.*, p. 413.
65. *Ibid.*, p. 392.
66. *Blue Flame*, p. 71.
67. *Ibid.*, p. 73.
68. *Ibid.*, p. 59.
69. *Ibid.*, p. 69.
70. Mikhail Naimy in his Arabic address to the Gibran International Festival in Beirut, 1970.
71. Naimy, *K.G.*, p. 195.
72. *Ibid.*, p. 207.
73. *Blue Flame*, p. xvii.
74. Quoted in J & K Gibran, p. 382.
75. Naimy, *K. G.*, p. 207.
76. *B.P.*, p. 435.
77. Naimy, *K.G.*, pp. 207–8.
78. Quoted in J & K Gibran, pp. 391–2.
79. *Ibid.*, pp. 392–3.
80. Naimy, *K.G.*, p. 260.
81. *Ibid.*, p. 255.
82. Kahlil Gibran, *Spirits Rebellious* tr. H. M. Nahmad (London, Heinemann 1973), pp. 103–4.
83. Kahlil Gibran, *The Prophet* (New York, Knopf 1963) p. 75.
84. *Ibid.*, p. 31.

85. *Ibid.*
86. *Ibid.*, p. 40.
87. Kahlil Gibran, *The Madman, His Parables and Poems* (London, Heinemann 1973), p. 56.
88. *The Prophet*, p. 68.
89. *Ibid.*, pp. 68–9.
90. The words are Philip Hitti's, quoted earlier (see note 64).
91. *Blake: Complete Writings*, ed. Geoffrey Keynes (Oxford, OUP 1966), p. 817.
92. *The Prophet*, p. 29.
93. *Blake*, p. 424.
94. *The Madman*, p. 9.
95. *Blake*, p. 540.
96. *The Madman*, p. 1.
97. *Blake*, p. 538.
98. *Ibid.*, p. 117.
99. *The Madman*, p. 58.
100. *Blake*, p. 218.
101. *The Prophet*. p. 72.
102. *Blake*, p. 151.
103. *The Prophet*, p. 35.
104. *Blake*, p. 214. The forest becomes the metaphor on which Gibran's long Arabic poem, *Al-Mawakib (The Procession)*, is built.
105. *B.P.*, p. 259.
106. *The Prophet*, p. 51.
107. *B.P.*, p. 88. It should be remembered that this was a period when Nietzsche's influence was much talked about.
108. Quoted in Naimy, *K. G.*, p. 124.
109. Kahlil Gibran, *The Forerunner: His Parables and Poems* (London, Heinemann 1974), p. 1.
110. *B.P.*, p. 86.
111. Mikhail Naimy, "Gibran at his peak", in *Gibran of Lebanon*, ed. S. B. Bushrui and Paul Gotch (Beirut, American University of Beirut 1975), p. 4.
112. *The Madman*, p. 1.
113. *Ibid.*, p. 45.
114. *Ibid.*, p. 49.
115. *Ibid.*, p. 63.
116. *Blue Flame*, p. 7.
117. *The Forerunner*, pp. 13–14.
118. *Ibid.*, p. 31.
119. *Ibid.*, pp. 58–59.
120. *Ibid.*, p. 61.
121. Kahlil Gibran, *Secrets of the Heart*, tr. Anthony R. Ferris, ed. Martin L. Wolf (New York, Signet 1975), p. 126.
122. *B.P.*, p. 303.

123. *Ibid.*, p. 326.
124. *Ibid.*, p. 353.
125. *The Prophet*, p. 10.
126. *Ibid.*, p. 9.
127. *Ibid.*, p. 96.
128. *Ibid.*, p. 4.
129. *Ibid.*, p. 10.
130. *Ibid.*, pp. 89–90.
131. *Ibid.*, pp. 13–14.
132. Freidrich Schiller, *On the Aesthetic Education of Man*, trans. Reginald Snell (London, Routledge & Kegan Paul 1954), pp. 108–9.
133. *The Prophet*, p. 41.
134. *Ibid.*, p. 67.
135. *Ibid.*, pp. 39–40. Gibran spells the word 'pigmy'.
136. *Ibid.*, p. 62.
137. *Ibid.*, p. 65.
138. *Ibid.*, p. 79.
139. *Blue Flame*, p. 9.
140. Kahlil Gibran, *Sand and Foam* (London, Heinemann 1974), p. 69.
141. *Ibid.*, p. 26.
142. *Ibid.*, p. 30.
143. *Ibid.*, p. 61.
144. *Ibid.*, p. 41.
145. *Secrets of the Heart*, pp. 102–3.
146. *Jesus, the Son of Man*, p. 63.
147. *Ibid.*, p. 192.
148. *Ibid.*, p. 46.
149. *Ibid.*, p. 43.
150. *Ibid.*, p. 2.
151. *Ibid.*, p. 63.
152. *Ibid.*, p. 100.
153. *Ibid.*, p. 106.
154. *Ibid.*, p. 111.
155. *Ibid.*, p. 136.
156. *B.P.*, p. 436.
157. *Ibid.*, p. 414.
158. *Ibid.*, p. 386.
159. Kahlil Gibran, *The Earth Gods* (London, Heinemann 1969), pp. 44–5.
160. *Ibid.*, p. 5.
161. *Ibid.*, p. 27–8.
162. *Ibid.*, p. 45.
163. It is not known when Gibran began work on *The Wanderer*. Most of the book appears to have been written during the last year of his life, but some parts of it possibly date from as much as a decade earlier (i.e. after publication of *The Forerunner*).

164. Kahlil Gibran, *The Wanderer: His Parables and His Sayings* (London, Heinemann 1969), pp. 88–9.
165. For example, Barbara Young's biography creates a legend of Gibran as a saintly primitivist.

BIBLIOGRAPHY

1. Works by Kahlil Gibran

a) Written directly in English

The Madman, New York, Alfred A. Knopf, 1918. (First British edition: London, William Heinemann, 1946.)

The Forerunner, New York, Alfred A. Knopf, 1920. (First British edition: London, William Heinemann, 1963.)

The Prophet, New York, Alfred A. Knopf, 1924. (First British edition: London, William Heinemann, 1926.)

Sand and Foam, New York, Alfred A. Knopf, 1926. (First British edition: London, William Heinemann, 1927.)

Jesus, the Son of Man: His Words, and His Deeds as Told and Recorded by Those who Knew Him, New York, Alfred A. Knopf, 1928. (First British edition: London, William Heinemann, 1954.)

The Earth Gods, New York, Alfred A. Knopf, 1931. (First British edition: London, William Heinemann, 1962.)

The Wanderer: His Parables and His Sayings, New York, Alfred A. Knopf, 1932. (First British edition: London, William Heinemann, 1965.)

The Garden of the Prophet, New York, Alfred A. Knopf, 1933. (First British edition: London, William Heinemann, 1954.)

Lazarus and His Beloved: A One-Act Play, edited with an introduction by the author's cousin and namesake Kahlil Gibran and his wife Mary Gibran, Greenwich (Connecticut), New York Philosophical Society, 1973. (First British edition: London, William Heinemann, 1973.)

Dramas of Life [*Lazarus and His Beloved* and *The Blind*], edited with an introduction by the author's cousin and namesake Kahlil Gibran and his wife Mary Gibran, Philadelphia, Westminster Press, 1982.

90

b) Translated from the Arabic

Between Night and Morn: a special selection, edited by Martin L. Wolf and translated by A. R. Ferris, New York, Wisdom Library, 1972.

The Broken Wings, translated by A. R. Ferris, New York, Citadel Press, 1957. (First British edition: London, William Heinemann, 1959).

Mirrors of the Soul, translated, and with biographical notes by Joseph Sheban, New York, Philosophical Library, 1965.

Nymphs of the Valley, translated by H. M. Nahmad, New York, Alfred A. Knopf, 1948. (First British edition: London, William Heinemann, 1948.)

The Procession, edited, translated, and with a biographical sketch by George Kheirallah, New York, The Wisdom Library (A Division of the Philosophical Library), 1958.

Prophecies of Love: Reflections from the Heart, selected by Julie Clardy, Kansas City, Hallmark Cards Inc., 1971.

The Prophet in Miniature, or Life in Procession, recreated, composed and rhymed by Lawrence T. Fares, Philadelphia, Dorrance, 1973.

Prose Poems, translated by Andrew Ghareeb, New York. Alfred A. Knopf, 1934. (First British edition: London, William Heinemann, 1964.)

Secrets of the Heart, translated by A. R. Ferris, New York, Philosophical Library, 1947.

Spirits Rebellious, translated by H. M. Nahmad, New York. Alfred A. Knopf, 1948. (First British edition: London, William Heinemann, 1949.)

Spiritual Sayings, translated and edited by A. R. Ferris, New York, Bantan, 1970.

A Tear and a Smile, translated by H. M. Nahmad, with an introduction by Robert Hillyer, New York, Alfred A. Knopf, 1950. (First British edition: London, William Heinemann, 1950.)

Tears and Laughter, translated by A. R. Ferris, New York, Philosophical Library, 1947.

Thoughts and Meditations, translated by A. R. Ferris, London, William Heinemann, 1961. (First American edition: New York, Citadel Press, 1961.)

A Treasury of Kahlil Gibran, edited by Martin L. Wolf and

translated by A. R. Ferris, New York, Citadel Press, 1951. (First British edition: London, William Heinemann, 1974.)

A Second Treasury of Kahlil Gibran, edited by Martin L. Wolf and translated by A. R. Ferris, New York, Citadel Press, 1962.

A Third Treasury of Kahlil Gibran, compiled by Andrew Dib Sherfan, Secaucus (NJ), Citadel Press, 1975.

The Voice of the Master, translated by A. R. Ferris, New York, Citadel Press, 1963. (First British edition: London, William Heinemann, 1960.)

The Wisdom of Gibran: Aphorisms and Maxims, edited and translated by Joseph Sheban, New York, Philosophical Library, 1966.

c) Art Works

Sculpture: Kahlil Gibran, with a foreward by Evan H. Turner, Boston, Bartlet Press, 1970.

Twenty Drawings, introduced by Alice Raphael, New York, Alfred A. Knopf, 1919.

2. Letters

Beloved Prophet: The Love Letters of Kahlil Gibran and Mary Haskell and Her Private Journal, edited and arranged by Virginia Hilu, New York, Alfred A. Knopf, 1972.

Blue Flame: The Love Letters of Kahlil Gibran to May Ziadah, translated and edited by Suheil B. Bushrui and Salma H. al-Kuzbari, Burnt Mill, Longman, 1983.

Kahlil Gibran: A Self-Portrait, translated from the Arabic and edited by A. R. Ferris, London, William Heinemann, 1960 (includes fifty letters).

Hawi, Kahlil S., *Kahlil Gibran: His Background, Character and Works*, Beirut, American University of Beirut, 1963 (includes four letters).

The Love Letters of Kahlil Gibran and Mary Haskell, arranged and edited by Annie Salem Otto, Houston, Annie Salem Otto, 1964.

Naimy, Mikhail, *Kahlil Gibran: His Life and his Work*, Beirut,

Khayat, 1964 (includes twenty-seven letters written to the author).

Otto, Annie Salem, *The Art of Kahlil Gibran*, Port Arthur, Texas, Hinds Printing Company, 1965 (includes four letters).

Unpublished Gibran Letters to Ameen Rihani, translated with an introduction by Suheil Badi Bushrui, Beirut, World Lebanese Cultural Union, [1972].

3. Biography and criticism

a) Books wholly devoted to Gibran

Abou Hamdeh, Said; Bushrui, Suheil B.; Munro, John M. and Smith, Marcus; *A Poet and his country: Gibran's Lebanon: A photo essay*, Beirut, Middle East Press Inc., 1970.

Bushrui, Suheil B. and Gotch, Paul, *Gibran of Lebanon: new papers*, Beirut, Librairie du Liban, 1975.

Bushrui, Suheil Badi, *An Introduction to Kahlil Gibran*, Beirut, Dar el-Mashreq, May 1970.

Bushrui, Suheil Badi, *Kahlil Gibran: An Introductory Survey of His Life and His Work*, Ibadan, University Press, 1966.

Bushrui, Suheil B. and Munro, John M., *Kahlil Gibran: Essays and Introductions*, Beirut, Rihani House, 1970.

Challita, Mansour, *Luttes et triomphe de Gibran*, Beirut, Editions Orient-Occident, 1970.

Daoudi, M. S., *The Meaning of Kahlil Gibran*, Secaucus (NJ), Citadel Press, 1982.

Gibran, Jean and Gibran, Kahlil [the poet's cousin and namesake], *Kahlil Gibran: His Life and World*, Boston, New York Graphic Society, 1974.

Ghougassian, Joseph P., *Kahlil Gibran: Wings of Thought*, New York Philosophical Library, 1973.

Hanna, Suheil Salim, *An Arab Expatriate in America*, Ph.D thesis, Indiana University, 1973.

Hawi, Kahlil S., *Kahlil Gibran: His Background, Character and Works*, Beirut, American University of Beirut, 1963. (Reprinted London, Third World Centre for Research and Publication, 1982.)

Huwayik, Yusef, *Gibran in Paris*, New York, Popular Library, 1976.

Naimy, Mikhail, *Kahlil Gibran: His Life and his Work*, Beirut, Khayat, 1964.

Otto, Annie Salem, *The Art of Kahlil Gibran*, Port Arthur, Texas, Hinds Printing Company, 1965.

Otto, Annie Salem, *The Parables of Kahlil Gibran: An Interpretation of his Writings and his Art*, New York, Citadel Press, 1963.

Ross, Martha Jean, *The Writings of Kahlil Gibran*, unpublished Master's thesis, The University of Texas, 1948.

Sherfan, Andrew Deeb, *Kahlil Gibran: The Nature of Love*, New York, Philosophical Library, 1971.

Young, Barbara, *This Man from Lebanon: A Study of Kahlil Gibran*, New York, Alfred A. Knopf, 1945.

b)   Books devoting some attention to Gibran's work or life

Bragdon, C. F., 'Modern Prophet from Lebanon, Kahlil Gibran,' *Merely Players*, New York, Alfred A. Knopf, 1929, 139–147.

Brockelmann, C., 'Die Moderne Arabische Litteratur,'' *Geschichte der Arabischen Litteratur* (dritter Supplementband,) Leiden, E. J. Brill, 1942, 457–471.

Gail, Marzieh, *Other People, Other Places*, Oxford, George Ronald, 1982, 227–231.

Khemiri, Tahir and Kampffmeyer, G., *Leaders in Contemporary Arabic Literature*, London, Trubnar, 1930, 17–19.

Russell, G. W. (AE), 'Kahlil Gibran,' *Living Torch*, New York, Macmillan, 1938, 168–169.

For a comprehensive bibliography, including Arabic works by and on Gibran, see Bushrui, Suheil Badi, *Kahlil Gibran: A Bibliography*, Beirut, Centenary Publications, 1983.